The Colorado Whoopenhollars

The Colorado Whoopenhollars

Living a Good Life Despite the Great Depression

Jean Rutherford Duaine

"God gave us
our memories so that
we might have roses
in December"
–J.M. Barrie

Copyright © 2009 by Jean Rutherford Duaine.

Library of Congress Control Number: 2009905049
ISBN: Hardcover   978-1-4415-2990-9
                Softcover   978-1-4415-2989-3

All rights reserved. No part of this book may be reproduced or transmitted in any form or by any means, electronic or mechanical, including photocopying, recording, or by any information storage and retrieval system, without permission in writing from the copyright owner.

This book was printed in the United States of America.

To order additional copies of this book, contact:
Xlibris Corporation
1-888-795-4274
www.Xlibris.com
Orders@Xlibris.com

Contents

Chapter One	Take Me Home Mountain Road	13
Chapter Two	Places And People	20
Chapter Three	Uptown	29
Chapter Four	School And Church	35
Chapter Five	Finding A House And Making It Home	41
Chapter Six	Good Old Summer Time	45
Chapter Seven	Daddy	51
Chapter Eight	Mamma	61
Chapter Nine	Making Ends Meet	66
Chapter Ten	Picnics, Berry Picking And Fishing	72
Chapter Eleven	More Summer Memories And An Addition To Our Family	76
Chapter Twelve	The Dangers We Faced	81
Chapter Thirteen	Learning To Be Responsible	86
Chapter Fourteen	Vegetables And Celebrations	89
Chapter Fifteen	Thanksgiving	97
Chapter Sixteen	Christmas	99

The rest of the Whoopenhollar Stories, written by Daddy- W.I. Rutherford.
A Documentation of Dates and Camps Where Rutherford Worked – Written by Michael I. Smith, Grandson
Histories Of Old Billy Rutherford, Our Dad, Bill Rutherford and a History of the Ecklund Family
Music-My Little Girl, Sam M. Lewis.

Dedicated to the loving memory
of

John Paul Rutherford
1930-1998

Johnny Whoopenhollar had to go on ahead of us
but he will be there to welcome the rest of us,
standing in the open door of our New Cabin

ACKNOWLEDGEMENTS

I AM ESPECIALLY grateful to you, Clarice Rutherford, writer and published author, (and my sister-in-law) for your confidence in my ability to write. We had all looked to you to write something of the Rutherford kids growing up in Georgetown that would wrap around the exciting adventure filled stories that Daddy made up. In 2006 you said to me, "Jean, you are the one who should write the story because you were there, I was not." I couldn't even imagine that I could take on that task. With your help, encouragement and your blessings I said I would try. Thank you Clair for believing in me. As I continued to work on this piece I could hear you saying, "Yes, you can do it."

Thank you, Mike, my youngest, who is also a writer and with a degree in American Studies. (Michael I. Smith) You believed in me, too and encouraged me every day for the past two years. I remember that quite awhile ago I felt a longing to be able to write and tell everyone what a wonderful mother I had. I so wanted to express my love for her and didn't know how to do it. I asked you, Mike if you would write it for me. Surely you would do it. She was your Grammie, and you were so close to her. You were unhesitant to reply. "No, Mom, you need to write it. It will come from the heart. Just get started and you will see." I was able to do it by writing about The Whoopenhollars. With great appreciation – thanks for all the knowledge you have of your Grandpa's days in the CCC's. It strikes me as so amazing, that I grew up under the umbrella of the Civilian Conservation Corps, and yet had so little knowledge of what Daddy was doing while I was growing up. Here you come, with an appetite for the history of that time and filled in all the blank pages for me.

Thank you Bruce (Rutherford), my nephew, for the knowledge you have of the history of our family. Just when I thought I had all the leaves and branches connected on this family tree of ours, you corrected me and put things right. I am grateful for the documentation you have done over the years. Thanks you, more than I can express for the addition of pictures to add to the text – you are truly a keeper of documents and family pictures. What a gift!

Thanks to you David (Rutherford) my nephew, for writing the music to a song that came out of the early 1900's. I remembered the tune and the words, just like Daddy sang to me. You had never heard it, but you listened while I sang it, wrote the score for me and I've included it in the book. Later you found it on line and confirmed that it was written by Sam M. Lewis in 1915.

To you dear brothers of mine – Bill, Buff and Glenn. I could not have written this book if you had not provided me with material. You're sister did little more than cling to Mamma's and Grandma's aprons. Since I was the only girl, I was given household chores to do, learning as I went. My growing up in the 1930's meant that I was only 10 years old when that era passed. The things that you boys did were far more adventurous than I was ever allowed. Thanks so much for telling me your stories and letting me tell it as if they were my memories. John has been gone now for ten years. I have felt very close to him as I recounted the part he played in all the stories. He would, like you, have had much to tell. We were all blessed for having had him to love and grow up with. His interests were many. He was a lover of history, especially the Civil War era, he loved music, travel and he was innovative in his work place and around his home. His family was absolutely his priority, and oh how he did love being a Grandpa.

I thank all of you in this wonderful family of ours for the interest you have shown and the encouragement you have given me. You have all seemed anxious for me to complete it. I hope you aren't disappointed, since you have waited so long.

I am especially grateful to my friends here in Circle City, my church family at First Presbyterian Church in Wickenburg, Arizona and loving friends all over these United States. You have all shown such a genuine interest in what I was writing. This encouragement is what kept me going. I am so appreciative of you, Dane Hewitt, like a grandson; for all that you've done when I needed help with computer problems and making disks. Thanks a big bunch.

I can not continue to give thanks without remembering the One who helped me the most. My Heavenly Father was with me every day that I picked up my pen, usually sitting at my kitchen table. He heard every prayer when I asked him to please help me. There were times when I actually sat down to write and I had not one thought to put on paper. Monday was my writing day, but that didn't mean that I knew what was going to transpire. I give God the Glory and the Praise. If you like what I've written, don't forget that it is to Him that you will give thanks.

I am your Sister, your Mother, your Grand mother, your Aunt, your Cousin, and your friend.

Blessings to all and with love, Jean

CHAPTER ONE

Take Me Home Mountain Road

EXCEPT FOR THE cuts in the rocky slopes of the valley, the mountains are just as I remember them as I travel west from Denver on Interstate 70. The road has certainly changed. The speed of the many cars and big trucks is not at all like it was back in the 1930's. In those days we followed a two lane, unpaved gravel road, taking twists and curves slowly as we went through Mt. Vernon Canyon and over Floyd Hill, then descending into Idaho Springs. The Highway U.S. 40 veered to the right to climb upward to Empire and travel on over Berthoud Pass, and veering to the left, became Highway U.S. 6. That would take us to Georgetown, Silver Plume and climb over Loveland Pass to the western side of the Continental Divide. There were many hairpin curves on the route, especially after you left Georgetown. It was a dangerous route to be taking and winter was treacherous. Loveland Pass was closed every winter, only open in summer and it was a narrow dirt road. It didn't become a year round route until the late 1930's.

William I. Rutherford-Loveland Pass 1926

Loveland Pass in the 1930's

We didn't travel much back then but when we did, it was only to Denver from our home in Georgetown; usually only once a year. That was a big event for us. Daddy took us in his 1929 Willys Whippet automobile on New Year's Day. When we got there, we would sit in the car until darkness took over, waiting for the anticipated event. Our parents got out of the car, keeping a close watch on all five of us and taking care that we remained together. We all stood on the sidewalk getting more excited with each passing minute. Oh my, when the Christmas lights finally were turned on, there before us were the Civic Center buildings so completely covered with lights that you would never be able to describe it to anyone and to add to the splendor of that, was the beautiful sound of Christmas Carols. They were the traditional Christmas Carols that we sang in church and in our school – you know, the ones that told of the birth of The Christ Child. On the grounds of these public buildings we saw larger than life size images of Mary and Joseph looking down at the baby Jesus in a manger. There were shepherds and angels! There were even sheep and cattle lying down close to the Holy Family.

The magnificence of the scene before us was so amazing and seemed so real to us that none of us could speak, only oohs and aahs, like music from wind instruments heard on the cold evening air. We had seen it all the year before and the year before that, and yet it was like a surprise, as though we were seeing it for the first time. I don't remember how long we stood there in the cold, filling our eyes with the magic of the lights, but when we children and Mamma had taken in enough of the bone chilling cold, Daddy would ask us if we were ready to head back home.

We hated to leave the sights and sounds of the city, which was still dressed in its Christmas finery, but Daddy knew that it would be late by the time we got home to Georgetown and there was the possibility that the weather might bring snow as we climbed from the mile high city, up into the foothills and then into the mountains. All five of us sat in the back seat, dressed in woolen coats and hats and long stockings. A car heater was not one of our luxuries. Snuggled close, due to the width of the seat, helped keep us warm.

Billy was the oldest and was always the one who knew to watch for things along the way. He kept us entertained as he speculated what we might be seeing from the back seat windows if it weren't so dark. Frankie, the next oldest, would wonder if there were any horses out there in the Genesse Park area where the buffalo herds were grazing. Johnny, my twin, myself and little brother Glenn were getting sleepy now and finding it very difficult to think about anything but being home. We were getting hungry, as well.

As we drove into Idaho Springs it began to snow, but the pretty lights on some of the houses and in the store windows became visible and now we seemed to become more awake than sleepy. Having the snow falling as we drove along watching the Christmas lights from the car windows, filled us once again with that excitement we had felt when we saw the sights of the city, but now we were seeing lights through snow flakes! As we left the little town and kept on going toward Georgetown, it began to snow harder.

Daddy was driving so carefully with his precious cargo and finally we came to the junction – only a few more miles to go now.

We were getting anxious to be out of that car so that we could move a little. Soon the snow was coming so hard and fast, swirling in the front of the car lights that it was enough to make you dizzy. Big, thick flakes began to stick to the windshield and the wipers could no longer keep the windshield cleared. Daddy would roll down his window and watch for the edge of the road on his side and Mamma would roll down her window and watch for the edge of the road on the right. With heads sticking out on both sides, they kept us from going off the road and into a ditch. With two windows rolled down, the cold night air filled the car. We little sardines in the back seat were unaware of any danger that can come from driving in a winter storm. We were very much awake at this point, complaining that we were cold. We remained sitting tight – I do mean tight, only asking "how much farther?" As we spoke we filled the cold air with our warm breath.

When we finally drove into our yard, close to the back door of our house, we were so glad to be home but we knew that when we piled out of the place that had partially kept us warm, we would experience the real cold. We would make a dash for the back door.

Once in the house, our parents would check the kitchen and dining room stoves for any hope of some lingering hot coals. They always banked the fires with large lumps of coal before leaving for any length of time.

It seemed chilly but in no time some added sticks of wood caught from the hot coals and before we knew it, there was a good fire for Mamma to cook us some supper.

Shedding our warm coats, hats and gloves or mittens, we were quite comfortable now.

Supper was good no matter what we had. We would never have stopped at a restaurant to eat before we drove home. Daddy could not have afforded that. He had made provision to fill the gas tank for our trip and that would be cost enough – it must have taken five gallons of gasoline for this marvelous outing, and at twenty cents a gallon, it was considered to be a special occasion.

* * *

Memories of how the road used to be come flooding back again. Mountains do change in one's life time, but only by the ways of man. The mountain on the west side of the narrow valley has been cut away to make a place for this Interstate 70. The hairpin curves are gone but that makes the grade going southwest to Silver Plume even steeper.

Georgetown 1940's

Highway 6 and Loop Railroad Bridge 1920's

I can leave all that traffic by taking the exit into Georgetown and begin watching for houses and places that hopefully, I'll recognize. I'm glad that the high, steep and rugged mountains that form the deep valley haven't changed, except for the west mountain that had to be cut away to widen the highway. The growth of the town is limited by the width of the valley. The south end is also protected by mountains. Only the north end can grow. As a matter of fact, it has grown, but is limited because of the beautiful lake and dam there.

* * *

Novelist Thomas Wolfe once wrote, "You can't go home again." But, I say "You can bring home back to you." When I want to go back home, I have to go back in my memories and bring home back to me. It won't be just the house where we lived, it will be the people in our lives that loved and nurtured us; our parents, grandparents, teachers, friends and neighbors. Why would I want to return to the place that held memories of growing up in a small mountain mining town and living a life of the consequences of The Great Depression? The answer to that lies in the fact that as children we did not know that we were deprived. We certainly weren't depressed. We were unaware of the hardships our parents suffered as they struggled to provide for us. We didn't understand why our father had to live apart from us so that he could earn a wage that would meet the daily needs of his family. We missed him terribly, but we never questioned why he couldn't be with us. His pay was small but Mamma was a good manager. She fed us good healthy meals and kept our clothes clean and mended.

The kids in our neighborhood had basically the same life style; however, there were some who seemed hungrier than we. Mamma taught us never to go outside eating something if we didn't have enough to share. If one of us would forget, and be eating an apple or an orange, you could bet that one of the neighborhood kids would say, "Dibs on the core" or "Dibs on the peel."

Even though Mamma cooked healthy meals, I know that often we didn't feel full. There were never leftovers. Everyone ate everything on his plate and was excused from the table after asking "Please may I be excused?" You just got used to never being filled up.

Of course we were poor, but we didn't know it. Looking back, I realize that we were very rich in everything that truly mattered.

CHAPTER TWO

Places and People

I LEAVE I-70 at the Georgetown exit. I think I'll go over to Rose Street so I can see the Ecklund house where our grandparents lived and where our family also lived for a short time. Billy and Frankie were little when the folks moved there, and Johnny, myself and Glenn were born in that house. I'll turn right at the stop sign and drive to the bridge, turn left, cross the bridge and turn right onto Rose Street. Of course the houses have changed some but not enough that I don't recognize them and remember who once lived in them.

Oh, there on my right is Auntie Berg's house. She wasn't really our aunt, but a very dear friend of our family and in those days we didn't call older people by their first names. We didn't even give them a title of Mr. or Mrs. if they were very close and dear friends. Her name was Louise Berg, a Swedish widow lady. She was very tall and straight as a yard stick. She had snow-white hair. I can even remember how good her house smelled and how clean and shiny everything was. She had pretty crocheted doilies on end tables and the side-board. The dining room table always had a white table cloth on it and a pretty china tea set. The aroma was coffee and many times included the sweet scent of cardamom, if she had just made sweet bread or Kringlor. Kringlor is a sweet bread dough, rolled in small ropes, twisted into shapes like a pretzel, sprinkled with coarse sugar and baked. The kitchen was so white, as I remember, because the cabinets reached to the high ceiling and they were all painted a high gloss white. The windows always sparkled because they were so clean, with white curtains framing the panes. It was a warm comforting place. I suppose her house was like this because there were no children there to make messes and leave sticky fingerprints on anything.

We always included Auntie Berg in our family holidays. Her husband died before I was born, as a result of the great flu epidemic that swept the country in 1918. One of their daughters, Hazel, died from the flu shortly after graduating high school in 1925.

She was Mamma's best friend. Mamma talked about Hazel a lot. I always felt sad when she talked about her because I knew she missed her.

Hazel Berg-Paul Ecklund-Ethel Ecklund 1922

Auntie Berg's other daughter, Helen, was the eldest and she was away at Nursing School in Denver – as children, we didn't get to know her well, until she finished school and would come to see her mother. Now a days people live in Georgetown and commute to Denver every day to go to work. Auntie Berg and Helen were such a meaningful part of our lives that we felt as though they were family. Auntie and Grandma Ecklund were very good friends. They seemed like sisters from Sweden.

Across the street is the north end of the park which covers a complete block. Oh, what memories the park has for all of us. It was our playground, as we grew up on the south east corner of it. I wish the boys were here with me now so they could see how it has changed since we played here. There is a beautiful gazebo north of the fountain. That didn't used to be here. If I close my eyes and listen, I think I can see and hear a brass band playing a John Philip Sousa March.

Another addition is some state of the art playground equipment like I've never seen here before. When we were children, it was just a pretty park with lots of old trees, a pretty fountain in the middle and wrought iron benches for sitting. The entire park is fenced with ornate wrought iron and impressive iron arches over all four-entry gates, one on each corner. The fence and gateways are original, dating back to 1891. In 2008, the entire fence was restored and the missing sections were duplicated to match the original design, which some locals call wire hair-pin fence.

The most vivid and wonderful memory I have of our activities in the park are of the golden days of autumn when the blue of the sky seemed even more blue than during the summer. Perhaps it was because of the brightness of the leaves from all the old cottonwood trees. Even though the ground was covered by them, for many days the trees seemed to keep a sufficient amount of their gorgeous dress, refusing to let all of the leaves fall and then stand there naked, as they are in winter. With bright yellow above us like a canopy and a carpet under our feet of the same hue, walking in it and kicking as we went, we would stay all day.

When the boys were older and stronger, they became innovators of what to do with dry fallen leaves. That resulted in their engineering abilities to be expressed. I am sure that God gave each of them the gift of building and repairing and it served them immeasurably all of their lives. From the golden days in the park, "Leaf Houses" were born! Good thing the boys had become strong because they had to carry some of the wrought iron benches to the spot where the leaf house would be built. The blueprint in their minds called for four benches to make the framework – that would be the walls. A place was left open for the door. The roof was made by lifting two more benches and laying them across the four that were already in place. This addition was the roof. Most of the time our outdoor activities included our neighborhood friends: The Katzenmeyers, Rockwells, and Johnsons. At this stage of the development of the leaf house, I was asked to join in and so was my friend Geneva Frank, who lived across the street from us.

Now was the time to rake leaves, gather them in bushel baskets and bring them to the building site. The benches had to have leaves packed very tightly into all of the spaces until it was compact. The opening left for a door was only accessible on hands and knees.

Once inside the house you could only sit and there was only enough room for only three or four of us at a time. There was nothing to do once inside but to enjoy the accomplishment and feel cozy. I can still remember the smell of the dry leaves as I reminisce. One of us would run home just across the street and ask Mamma if we could have some graham crackers so we could eat in our new little hut. Of course she said "yes." Once, not so long ago, Glenn told me that he and his friends were still building leaf houses in the early 1940's. I don't know how they were able to get cigarettes, but they did and they tried smoking them in their little house made of dry leaves! I said to him "You could have set it all on fire and been burned up – what were you thinking? You should have stuck with graham crackers." I remember how he laughed at me!

Leaving the park scene and continuing south to 927 Rose Street, I come to Grandpa and Grandma Ecklund's house where I was headed all the time, but got side tracked as I remembered Auntie Berg's house and the park. The Ecklund House looks like a duplex, and it was just that, when it was built by two brothers named Joe and Bob Church in 1876. It was still a duplex until some time in the 1950's. Grandpa and Grandma and their two children – Ethel (Mamma) and Paul (Uncle Paul), bought the house in 1922. They lived in the south side and rented out the other side.

In 1929 Daddy and Mamma with two little ones – Billy, fifteen months and Frankie, a new baby, moved into the renters side. Daddy had lost his livery business and their house on Taos St. next door to the Old Missouri Fire House to the north, because of the Crash – that's when the banks closed their doors and the Great Depression started. My, how that must have hurt Daddy. He had his own business when he asked Mamma to marry him, even had a house for her. Now he had no way to provide for his little family and no place to live. After moving to the duplex, Daddy got a job working as a truck driver for Clear Creek County. In 1930 Johnny and I were born, in August of 1932 along came Glenn.

By this time the little place was pretty packed and very lively. On each side of the house was a kitchen, dining room and a living room. Upstairs on each side were two very small bedrooms. There were no bathrooms but there was an out house in the back yard that hung over the creek. We were no different from many of the town residents. The more elaborate houses had indoor plumbing and that was considered "very modern" and a luxury.

I have no memory of living in the Ecklund duplex, because I was so little when we moved out of it, however I have many memories of spending time there. Their yards, front and back were always so pretty and well kept. I never see a yellow rose bush without thinking of the one that grew by the kitchen door and perhaps my love of pansies come from the memory I have of Grandma's big pansy bed in the front yard. There were hollyhocks by the dining room window. Mamma showed me how to make southern ladies in pretty ball room gowns by using one blossom, a bud and a tooth pick. There were bleeding heart plants along the walk way and in front of the living room windows. In the back yard along the fence by the creek were sweet peas.

They had a nice vegetable garden as well and the best things there were the Swedish peas. They were a little sweeter and more tender than the regular peas and Grandma would cook them in their pods and serve them in a delicious cream sauce. She was such a good cook and a marvelous baker. I can still see how the kitchen looked with the black cook stove heated by coal and wood. I believe that I can still remember how it smelled, as well. There was always coffee in a pot at the back of the stove keeping warm for whom-ever stopped by. Even as children, we were given coffee with cream and sugar.

Jean John Frank and Billy-Ecklund's Yard 1933

After we moved from there, we loved to run an errand for Mamma; taking something to Grandma or to borrow something, because it most certainly meant a cup of coffee and a big soft sugar cookie. Grandma always made them filled – two cookies with a nice raisin filling between, or we might have a Kringlor. Then, if it were summer, we didn't return home without a bouquet of yellow roses, pansies or sweet peas to take to Mamma. Grandpa spent most of his time working in his old shed. He had been a blacksmith in the mines when he was employed, but I remember him only as being retired. He had a forge in his shed and was usually sharpening steel. His work was considered excellent and he could get contracts with the mines to do their steel sharpening at home. It was fun to go in his private work place. It always seemed so dark in there. We could watch the sparks fly when he was grinding steel on the big wheel. He would let the boys turn the crank on the bellows to keep the fire hot in the forge. When I was in there, I didn't do that, I just watched. Grandpa would stop every once in a while and go to the wall on the east side of the shed and look out of a tiny little window he had put in there; "Grandpa, what are you looking at?" Little Glenn would ask him "I'm keeping an eye on Teddy," he would reply. "Why do you have to do that?" "Because I want to make sure that he is still in the front yard and not gone off somewhere." Teddy was their dog. He was of no particular breed – just a dog, medium build and reddish brown in color. Teddy liked to chase cars when they went past his house going south. One day he got one foot run over and he was crippled in that foot the rest of his life. His foot healed but he continued to chase cars.

Frank Emma and Teddy 1938

Buff (Frankie) has Grandpa's forge and uses it occasionally, as he works with old horse-shoes, heating them for shaping into his works of art called "Sculpshoes."Grandpa was a gifted carpenter as well as a blacksmith. Doing carpentry was just another way of making ends meet. As children, we thought Grandpa could do anything and everything! He did the fixing and repairing around our house to help Mamma, and he also was an excellent shoe repairman. During the Depression, our family tried to make everything last as long as possible. Grandpa kept our shoes resoled and that way the shoes could be passed down to the next child that they would fit.

I don't ever remember him getting upset with us. It seems that he was a very patient, rather quiet and gentle grandpa. He suffered from a heart problem and was sickly quite often. I can remember going to his house and finding him asleep in his chair in the kitchen.

There were no Lazy Boy recliners in those days. He just rested from his work in a kitchen Captain's Chair. I remember the four legs had baling wire strung from one leg diagonally to another leg. That was just another one of the signs of the times. The drilled holes for the legs were so worn that even glue would not keep the legs tight. It was a method used to make the chair last. I remember seeing furniture legs like that in many homes, including ours! I don't remember Grandpa with hair. He was bald as far as I can remember. I've seen pictures of him at the time he married Grandma and he had a beautiful head of hair with some wave to it. He was a handsome man. I only remember him as seeming very old; however, he was only sixty-seven when he died of congestive heart failure in a hospital in Denver on December 7, 1941. That day was Sunday. The five of us were told, after we came home from Sunday School, that two things had happened that morning – our country was at war because the Japanese had bombed Pearl Harbor and that Grandpa had died. I didn't understand why or care that our country was at war. I saw no evidence of it where I stood listening, but I certainly understood that my Grandpa had died. As I think back now, here in front of this place that is so dear to me, I know that was the very first time that I felt sadness and loss. His funeral was heart wrenching for me. I was tall enough to see into the casket. He looked like he was asleep and as I wept I clung to the side and Mamma had to pry my grip loose when it was time to leave and go out of the church. I had been to other funerals with Mamma but this was much different.

Grandpa had taught us all, useful things that boys were interested in about fixing things, spading a garden, how to plant potatoes, digging for worms for fishing, planing a piece of lumber; oh, so many things. He taught me the correct way to do dishes. On washday at our house, Grandma came to help and I would go to their house to have lunch with Grandpa. I wasn't old enough to help with laundry, neither was I old enough to fix lunch for the two of us. I must have been sent there so that Grandpa wouldn't be alone all day. I enjoyed spending the day with him and that's when he taught me how to do dishes. I was already doing dishes by age six, but Mamma didn't have time to correct my method. Grandpa gave me precise instructions of how to turn a dish or cup over so the rinse water would drain off. I had to teach Johnny the right way because he and I were the breakfast dish washers at home.

We were so blessed to grow up living just a block away from our grandparents and our only uncle – Uncle Paul. What a loving young man he was and so devoted to all of us. He got a job working for Public Service right out of high school. I remember Grandma packing a lunch for him and one or two of us would walk to the Public Service plant to take it to him. It was so loud in there that we couldn't hear each other talk. He told us, in a very loud voice, what all of the switches, levers and lights were for as he explained the way the water wheel was producing electricity to our homes.

When the five of us were very young, he had a Model "A" Ford coupe with a rumble seat and he would let us sit back there and take us for little rides around town. Once when Frankie was riding next to him in the front, Uncle Paul went around a corner and the passenger side door was not closed tight, so Frankie fell out on the street. He wasn't hurt but it sure scared Uncle Paul.

Uncle Paul Ecklund and the Rutherford Kids-1938

The memories of Grandma, Grandpa and Uncle Paul and the Ecklund House are so wonderful, I could stay here on Rose Street and reminisce the rest of the day, but I want to get on up the street to see if I'm in for a surprise that could be disappointing or is it going to be another journey of the heart – a glad heart! Remember, it was said that you can't ever go back home; it just won't be the same – but you can bring home back to you!

CHAPTER THREE

Uptown

AFTER LEAVING GRANDMA and Grandpa's house, at 927 Rose St., I remember Susie Abrahamson, right across the street, on the bank of South Clear Creek. Her son, Tommy, was a prisoner of war in Germany in WWII. I can picture her sitting on her porch in a rocking chair. She liked to watch cars go by and visit with people walking by her house.

Right next door to Grandpa and Grandma's was the Faris house. Dr. and Mrs. Faris and their grown son and daughter, John and Mary lived in Denver. Father and son were dentists. They came to Georgetown on weekends in the summer and holidays through out the year. Dr. Faris senior always had treats for the five of us. He was especially fond of Glenn. Maybe that's because Glenn's middle name was Faris, named for the Doctor. I remember him telling Glenn to roll up the edge of his sweater all around and then Dr. Faris would start filling the cuff with candy. The rule was – the first time a candy fell out, that would be the end of the treat giving. Strange, now that I think about it, that the dentist who checked our teeth would lavish candy on us.

We also liked to go to their house when word got to us, a block away, that "The Faris's are up from Denver," because Dr. Faris made Root Beer and we always got to have some. That was a treat on a hot summer day because there was never enough money in Mamma's budget to buy Root Beer or any other kind of soda pop.

I had one tooth, the eyetooth, that was not straight, but the rest of my second teeth had come in very straight. Dr. John, the son, told me that if I'd keep pushing on that tooth it would gradually go into its proper place. He told me, "Jean, if you will work at straightening that tooth, I will buy you an ice cream soda." I don't remember how we got to Denver that summer, about a year later, probably with Uncle Paul. Dr. Faris' dentist office was in the Republic Building down town. There was a Drug Store on the main floor and after Dr. John saw how much straighter my tooth was, he took me down stairs to the Drug Store and bought me my very first Ice Cream Soda – it was strawberry. Young Dr. Faris was a very special person in my life. I remember that we sat on high stools at the marble counter. What a wonderful day it was! I was particularly fond of his sister Mary, as well, and always looked forward to seeing her. When I was in sixth grade, she knitted a beautiful sweater for me as a gift.

The Faris' told Mamma that it would be O.K. for us kids to pick dandelion greens in their yard for our rabbits. It seems to me that it was one of the best dandelion patches in Georgetown, at least in our part of town where we were allowed to go. One summer day, Johnny and I took a gunny sack and off we went to work. It wasn't something we just loved to do. We all had chores that had to be done and finding food for the rabbits that we raised for meat, was one of the chores.

When we got to Faris's house we looked at the swing on the big porch and as the minds of twins will do – we were thinking the same thing! We climbed up in it, not so easy with short legs, but we made it. "Jean, let's see how high this thing will go," Johnny said. "Oh, don't make it go too high, Johnny, cause I get scared," I replied. "OK, I don't want you going home and telling Mamma that I scared you, cause then she will scold me." That was probably so. We played on the swing for some time and when some kids our age came by and saw us they joined in and we forgot all about why we were there.

Soon our stomachs told us that it was lunchtime. Back then, nobody had snacks between meals. Three squares a day – that was it! "Johnny, we have to go home now, I'm hungry, aren't you?" "Yes, I am hungry, but we don't have any dandelions in the sack yet. We don't have time to pick a bag full and Mamma will worry about us if we don't get home at lunch time, – I've got an idea," Johnny said. "Let's go over behind Grandma's house and find some big rocks by the creek – we won't get down close to the water. We can put a lot of rocks in the sack and then put some dandelion greens on top of the bag." "Well, if you think that is OK, I guess we could do it," I said. We followed through with the plan, being careful by the creek, but the sack was so heavy that we had to drag it home. When we got it to the back door and announced to Mamma that we were home and hungry she came out to see how full the gunnysack was. Of course, she was expecting to find it full of nice green food for the rabbits. The whole thing looked pretty suspicious to her and when she checked, she found that there were big holes in the bottom of the sack. Funny that the two of us hadn't noticed rocks in the street behind us.

Mamma looked disgusted and disappointed in us. She probably thought about not giving us any lunch. That would be a pretty fair sentence. Because she was such a good mother and we needed food at mealtime, we were allowed to go to the table. I remember working in the hot sun all afternoon to get a new sack full of dandelions. How much better it would have been if we'd done it in the cool part of the day – but on the other hand the fun in the swing was also nice in the cool of the day. I don't remember ever pulling a stunt like that again, and what a lesson it taught us. Learning that to do it right, and using our heads, so we won't do stupid things, is the best way.

Continuing on, I see more old houses of people I knew in my childhood – both sides of the street bring back memories. There is the old house with the beautiful Silver Plume granite wall. The house looks very neglected now. In the 1930's a family named Havens lived in it. Earl and Mildred Smith, and their children, Pat and Allan, bought it in the late 30's. Well, there on the west side of the street is a beautifully kept home where Mrs. McFarland lived. We used to pick the crab apples from her tree in the front yard. I realize now, that this is one of the houses that was used in the filming of John Denver's movie in 1986 – "The Christmas

Gift." It really is a beautiful structure at 915 Rose Street. In the movie, it is where the postmistress lived and John Denver, who played George Billings, fell in love with her.

Now I see Mrs. White's house, it too, is looking magnificent – well kept. I see that it has a sign in the yard. It belongs to Historic Georgetown Inc. and is known as the Bowman-White House; that tells the history of it. Mrs. White was such a kind lady. Oh my, every house I see, I can recall things about their dwellers. There, as I drive slowly, I remember the house at 808 Rose, the Catholic Rectory. The priest's name was Father Walsh and he was not at all tolerant of children. We were afraid to go by the rectory. Billy crossed the empty lot north of Father Walsh's place, pulling his wagon up town when the priest came out and told him to get himself and his wagon off of his property – that his wagon made too much noise! He probably knew that Billy was a Presbyterian!!

Getting closer to where the businesses are, I see the John Buckley home where his wife Ivy and children Phyllis and Leroy lived. Ivy had a beautiful yard and wonderful sweet peas that climbed on a very large trellis. The blossoms were so fragrant you could smell them as you passed by on the sidewalk.

Across the street, is the house where Dr. Kirby lived and had his office. He is the Doctor that delivered both Billy and Frankie, in the Bieser house where the folks lived before I was born. After they moved to the Ecklund house, Dr. Kirby delivered Glenn. Johnny and I were born on a night when Dr. Kirby was out of town and his colleague, Dr. John Atchison, Jr. answered the call. I think he had to come from Idaho Springs, as there were not two doctors in Georgetown. Dr. John, as Mamma called him got more than he bargained for that night. The folks didn't know that Mamma was carrying twins until Dr. John delivered me; looked at Daddy, and told him that another baby was yet to be born. The shock was too much – Daddy fainted flat away. Grandma Rutherford was there, as the mid-wife. She quickly administered the smelling salts that the Doctor handed her, got Daddy back on his feet and proceeded with more directions from Dr. John. It was almost a half an hour before Johnny was delivered, but there was a problem. The Doctor couldn't get the baby to open up his lungs and give a lusty cry.

Grandma Rutherford followed the good Doctor's orders, which were: get two tubs of water. One must have very warm water in it, but not too hot and the other must contain ice cold water. Dr. John dunked little baby Johnny, five pounds, first in the warm water, then a quick dunk in the cold water, followed by holding him by the ankles and the neck and squeezing his little body like an accordion. The dunking and squeezing had to be repeated over and over, as those in the room prayed for Johnny to give a good healthy cry.

Prayers were answered that night but for a few days, baby Johnny hurt all over from that shock treatment. Mamma told me that for a few days, he moaned a lot in his little basket. I'll just bet that Dr. John Atchison had a lot to tell Dr. Kirby when he got back to town!

Johnny was given the name John Paul; for the Doctor who wouldn't give up on him, and for Uncle Paul. I was named Emma Jean, for Grandma Emma and because Jean went well with the name of my twin, John.

Just up the street from Dr. Kirby, is the Buckley Garage and gas station. It is closed now, but the building is being cared for by the younger generation of Buckley's. It serves now, as a reminder of how it used to be when the friendly face of John, and then son Leroy, would greet you, check your car's oil and wash your windshield, as the gas was pumping.

At the corner of Rose and 6th Streets, I see all of the building I remember as a child and places where we were sent on errands for Mamma. There is the Library. It is such a nice building – built in 1924. That is when Mamma was a Junior in High School. As a child, I thought it was an old building. We all liked going there to check out books, and once a week, as a Camp Fire Girl, I joined other girls in the basement for our meetings. I didn't go to the library when I was little; that was to come later on, in the 1940's. I loved to read the Nancy Drew Mysteries for girls.

Mr. A.G. Klein's Red and White Store is now a cafe. Kneisel and Anderson's family owned and operated, grocery-hardware store, looks very much as it did in the 1930's. It has been "kept up" as we say. All of the other buildings going east on 6th street have been restored and have nice shops in them. How good it is to see the change from the way it looked during the Great Depression and even into the 1940's. There were so many old empty buildings back then. My goodness – even a bank!! The

Bank of Georgetown closed its doors in 1933 when the financial crash hit our country. It would be over forty years before interested investors would get a charter to open another one.

Coming to the corners of 6th and Taos Streets, I'll go north on Taos so that I can soon be where we used to live.

CHAPTER FOUR

School and Church

THE TWO OUTSTANDING buildings on my way, are the school and the First Presbyterian Church, both of which were a major part of our growing up.

The Old School seems to be going through a restoration. It is very old – built in 1874. It is still a magnificent, bold, two storied structure made of red brick. Mamma started first grade there in 1913 and graduated from the High School in 1925. Uncle Paul started school in 1918 and graduated High School in 1930, a month after Johnny and I were born. I wonder if Mamma got to see her brother graduate? I'm sure she was very busy with the care of new twins and two other little ones under three and a half years old. Grandma couldn't have taken care of us, because she and Grandpa would have wanted to see their only son graduate. If Daddy was home, could he have been there to take care of us? I wish I had thought to ask Mamma.

All five of us also attended the same school for a portion of our education. We were all taught by Miss Mattie Oklun who was also Mamma and Uncle Paul's first through third grade teacher. In 1939, The WPA, a work force created by President Roosevelt's New Deal, built a new school where the old Barton Hotel had stood on the hill at the south end of Taos Street for many decades. The Old School was closed but each one of us could lay claim to beginning our grade school years in "Mamma's and Uncle Paul's School."

Georgetown School 1874-1939

Ethel Ecklund 8th Grade Graduation 1921

Billy finished 6th grade, Frankie finished 5th grade, Johnny and I, third grade and Glenn can proudly declare "me too," as he attended first grade there before the school closed. As little folks, we always thought that the up stairs of the school was called High School because of its location.

One day, probably about 1937, I was at recess, swinging in a swing on the school playground. I had learned to pump and I was quite high when I saw Mamma walking by the school on her way up town. Being surprised and happy to see her, I wanted the swing to stop so that I could go to her. In trying to get out of the swing while it was still in motion, I fell in the dirt and cut my right knee quite deeply. I remember that it bled a lot. If Mamma was able to complete her errand, or if she had to take me home for getting patched up, I don't recall. I still have a scar to help me remember it. I wonder if Mamma ever thought of taking a different street to go on her errands – just in case?

Across the street from the Old School is the First Presbyterian Church, also built in 1874. It is referred to now, as "The Little Stone Church By The Stream." It looks almost the same to me because it has been lovingly cared for over the years. However, in the late 40's an addition was made on the south side for Sunday School rooms. That was a gift from Frank and Vivian Kammerdiener who lived in Kansas City, Missouri and summered in Georgetown with their children. Our families united when Johnny married their daughter Glena in 1951. Along the sidewalk, on both sides are flower gardens, built and planted in 1965. The gardens are a place of beauty and sweet remembrance; a memorial for Judy Rutherford, taken from our family to be with God, when she was only seven years old. Judy is the daughter of Buff and Mary Lou.

In 2004 the church members and the town came together to celebrate a major restoration and one hundred thirty years of continuous service. First Presbyterian church was always our place of worship and learning the Bible.

On Sunday, October 2, 1938, when Johnny and I were eight years old, we were all baptized. Daddy was not there with us, as we stood with Mamma while Rev. Liggitt sprinkled each one of us. The water ran down our faces and we all giggled. Once again we had caused our mother embarrassment. This sort of behavior was not unusual in the House of the Lord.

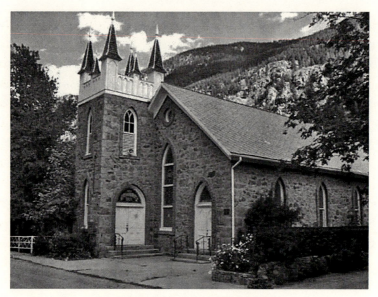
Georgetown Presbyterian Church

Grandpa and Grandma Ecklund and Uncle Charles and Aunt Marie Johnson always sat together on the left side of the sanctuary – that would be creek side. Mamma and her little band of hooligans sat in the pew about two aisles behind the older folks. With nothing to do but listen to sermons that we didn't understand, we were expected to sit quietly with our hands in our laps. We could hold to those rules for only ten or fifteen minutes at the very most. Seeing something that could cause distraction and usually hilarity was sure to happen. Billy nudged Frankie and whispered to him, "Look at the fly on Uncle Charles's head." Looking at both Uncle Charles and Grandpa's shiny baldheads, they watched the fly go from one to the other. Now apparently, the men were so intense as they listened to the sermon that they weren't even distracted by the tickle of a fly. Neither of them even gave a wave of the hand to shoo the fly away as it went from one shiny dome to the other.

Frankie poked Johnny and whispered, "Look at that fly on Grandpa's head." The whisper was loud enough that Jean heard it (that would be me) and we all started giggling. I passed it on to Glenn. Now there were five of us being entertained by a fly who seemed to be ice skating on the shiniest heads in the congregation. We tried to muffle our laughter as we looked at Mamma and saw "The Look" we were getting from her. Why is it that if something strikes you funny in church, you absolutely cannot get control of it?

I don't remember being in a Sunday School class for kindergarten or grade school ages. I only remember being taught by Mrs. Ona Anderson when I was a pre-teen. It was a class of girls. She was a good teacher and that is when I started to learn about Jesus and His teachings. One of the Public School teachers, Mr. Patterson, taught the boys class.

There was a Ladies Aid Society within the church and Mamma and Grandma were members. When it came time for them to take their turns at having the meeting and refreshments, they did it jointly. I helped as much as I could. There was a great deal of cleaning and polishing to do in the preparation for the gathering in our home. I remember that I liked doing it. It seemed like "being dressed up, to entertain". I suppose that is because it was so different than an ordinary day. I don't know what the boys did while the Ladies Aid Society met. Hum-m, it makes me wonder where those rowdies were.

I have wonderful memories of our beautiful old church by the creek. It was founded by Sheldon Jackson, an itinerant preacher who rode into Georgetown in 1869, found a small group of former Presbyterian folks and together they established a congregation. Five years later the stone church was dedicated. I must leave this serene place on Taos Street where there is the sound of the creek as it flows and rushes over the rocks and under a bridge. It wends its way farther north to meet up with the other fork of Clear Creek by Grandma and Grandpa's house.

Crossing 9th Street, right on the corner is Our Lady of Lourdes Catholic Church. It looks the same, which means that it has always been well cared for by its parishioners. Now I can see all of the houses in our block that made up "our neighborhood." There is Mr. and Mrs. Nelson's house and next door was where Mrs. Stephens lived. The Nelsons were Swedes and friends of our family. Mrs. Stephens was a tiny little lady, very sweet, who lived by herself for several years after the death of her husband; however, I do remember him. His name was Link. Mrs. Stephens and Mamma used to visit over the fence between our yards. Afraid of missing something, I was always beside my mother as she visited her and any of the neighbors – like Mrs. Katzenmeyer across the back fence.

Across the street from Nelson's house was Mrs. Pulcifer, a widow who gave piano lessons. Our Aunt Nona bought us a piano so that Johnny and I could take lessons. We went to her house every Saturday. I don't remember if they were for a half hour or a full hour, but I do remember that each lesson was fifty cents. Aunt Nona told us she would not pay out that kind of money if we didn't faithfully practice. If we failed to practice, then for sure our lessons would end. Mrs. Pulcifer had recitals in her home where each of her students played for their parents. It was always in the spring of the year. She served little refreshments, which I thought was all very lovely – like going to tea. I would have worn my best Sunday School dress and Johnny wore his best as well.

We would play a duet. I don't remember that I was especially good, but I remember that Johnny got praise from her. Playing the piano was supposed to help him straighten and strengthen his left hand and fingers which were withered from the surgery to his elbow after breaking it. I think she saw potential in both of us but we weren't good about practicing.

Our piano was in the living room, which wasn't heated in the winter. When we went in there to practice after school, we would have to wear a coat. It wasn't much fun and just another irritant for Mamma. She used to be at us all the time to practice so that we'd be ready for our next lesson. We would take turns going in the icebox, play one piece, come out and ask if our time was up yet! My explanation for never learning to play well has always been "I couldn't reach an octave with my mittens on." After about two years and we weren't able to play something well for Aunt Nona, she kept her promise about not paying Mrs. Pulcifer another fifty cents.

CHAPTER FIVE

Finding A House And Making It Home

HERE I AM at the N.E. corner of 10th and Taos Streets. Here is the house where we grew up! Now the days of childhood come upon me like an avalanche of memories. I'll have to sort them out. Where shall I start? I believe the best place to do that is to remember the day that I first saw the house. That is also the very first recollection I have of anything at all. It was the summer of 1933.

I remember that it was a warm sunny day. Johnny and I were three years old in April. Daddy left the month before, to go to his new job, working for the U.S. Forest Service in a CCC camp far away from us. He was hired to supervise the young enrollees of the Civilian Conservation Corps. This program was part of our President Franklin Delano Roosevelt's New Deal. It was a God send for millions of people out of work. Daddy wouldn't be able to live at home anymore because the CCC camps were not close to Georgetown. He was sent to Waunita Hot Springs in the southwest part of Colorado, near Gunnison. The rest of the 1930's would mean being without him. He would come home when he could, but it was only about every other month; five or six times a year. I remember, though, that we never celebrated a Christmas without him. I think that his supervisors understood that Daddy was a real, genuine family man and that he needed to be home with his five children and devoted wife. Daddy was an excellent employee of the U.S. Forest Service. He did his job well, worked hard and had an exceptional gift working and teaching young men.

Because we had outgrown the place where we lived in Grandma and Grandpa Ecklund's duplex, Mamma was out that day to look at the Presbyterian manse as a possible solution to our overcrowded living conditions. The Presbyterian Church never had a minister who lived in the manse. The church bought it for a rental income so they could keep the church maintained and pay a minister to come by train from Denver to deliver Sunday sermons. With four of us in tow and Mamma carrying baby Glenn, we walked to the house just a block away. There was another person with us, either to show mamma all of the rooms or perhaps it was a friend who came along to help her with all of us kids. Entering the house, it seemed so big – like a mansion, to us. It even had a bathroom!

As Mamma and the other lady talked, Johnny and I discovered a little cupboard under the kitchen window on the south side. It was constructed of wains coating and had a little door with a latch. Johnny and I played well together all of our childhood so it isn't surprising that we came up with a game to play when we found the cupboard.

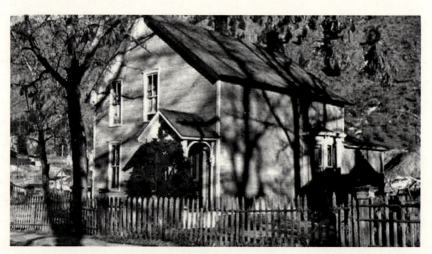

Rutherford Home-Presbyterian Manse-Christmas 1947

Immediately it spoke to both of us – Ah-ha, a hiding place and so the game began. We took turns going in and the other one would close the door. There was no room to move, just the right size for a three year old, on hands and knees until the one inside said, "let me out." Being caught up in the thought of actually working in this spacious kitchen, Mamma must have been swept away, to the point of not "watching her children." When she didn't see Johnny with me she looked as though she had just awakened and with concern, she said, "Jean, where is Johnny?" I began to laugh and then I opened the little door and showed her where he was. Mamma laughed then and so did the lady that was with her. While we played our game and Mamma gathered ideas of how our family and few belongings would adapt to this spacious house, Billy and Frankie, who were ages six and five had disappeared. "Now, where are they?" Mamma asked.

They had gone upstairs to investigate the big bedroom, two smaller ones and one big closet. Coming to the top of the stairs, they saw the staircase and realized what fun a banister could be. They had never slid down one before, but they did what seemed to be the right thing to do that beautiful day. After that, that's all they wanted to do. Mamma had to put a stop to it. It's strange that I only remember that particular day. I have no recollection of moving in. I wish that I did. I wonder if Uncle Paul moved our clothes, dishes, bedding and other household items in his Model A Ford car. Grandpa didn't ever drive, so I know that he couldn't have done it. He walked everywhere he went. I know we moved when Daddy was away at CCC camp and perhaps the first time he came home, Voila', there we were in our nice big house! I don't think it was a burden for him, but hopefully a joy. The rent was $10.00 a month, but that was relative to his salary.

In October of that year, Daddy asked Uncle Paul to bring Mamma, Billy and Frankie by car to come and see him in his CCC camp at Waunita Hot Springs. It was very important to him that his family would see for themselves where he worked and what kind of work he was doing. He was so proud of his family that I think maybe he was anxious to have his supervisors meet them. Because he couldn't be with us, I think also, that he thought if the oldest of us – Billy and Frankie could see for themselves just where he was and what it looked like in his camp, it would help them to understand his absence from them a little better. Johnny and I were only three and Glenn was just a year old. I suppose Grandma and Grandpa took care of the three of us so that this trip was possible. Boy, they must have had their hands full. I've thought so many times how much they meant to us. They were always there to help. How would Mamma have managed without them. We were so blessed!

Billy told me once about that trip to Waunita Hot Springs. He said that all of them stayed in a little house in town – not where the CCC camp was. He particularly remembered that there was a dump site right next door to the house. Wow! What treasures there might be there! Sure enough – he found an old clock that someone had thrown away. He got it and found time to take it apart and put it back together again while he was there. Billy loved to do things like that; he always wanted to know how things worked. He couldn't have been any happier if Mamma had had the money to take him to a store and buy him a new toy. He also remembered that Uncle Paul fished on the Gunnison River while they were there and he and Frankie were with him. Uncle Paul just loved to fish. I think that he always had his pole with line and hooks and bait with him wherever he went. That must have been the first time that the boys had ever been outside of Clear Creek County to go fishing.

Billy Paul Ethel Frank and Bill with Forest Supervisors
Waunita Hot Springs CCC Camp October 1933

CHAPTER SIX

Good Old Summer Time

SUMMER DAYS WERE happy and carefree for the five of us, but at my age now and looking back I wonder how Mamma kept her sanity. Little children always running in and out, the kitchen screen door constantly banging. There was much chatter, some delightful sounds of laughing, some crying and complaining and quite a lot of tattling. There was no game plan or organization for the way a day was going to go. Every day just played out according to the problems that arose; the weather, the temperament or illness of any of the children, or interruptions for Mamma.

Johnny and I had the job of doing the breakfast dishes. We had to stand on chairs to reach the sink. We didn't mind having this assignment because we loved playing in the water and using more soap than was necessary. We were unsupervised, as Mamma was busy with many tasks. We made lots of bubbles by drawing the bottlebrush in and out of the milk bottles to make sure we had them clean enough to return to the dairy. This sort of play caused water and soap to make a general mess out of things in that corner of the kitchen. Mamma would eventually stop

Frank Billy John Glenn Jean
The "Fabulous Five" in the Backyard 1935

the fun we were having and move us on to another chore; but of course we weren't happy about that. Oh well, tomorrow would be another day with more breakfast dishes. We didn't do supper dishes until we were a little older and a little taller.

Billy and Frankie built dams and roads in the back yard and played with their trucks. This kind of construction meant using the garden hose to make mud. It also meant going in and out of the house bringing in mud, to find a certain large cooking spoon or any one of Mamma's kitchen tools. Those items were eventually returned to the drawer where they belonged when the boys were told to go and find them because Mamma needed them. Glenn was too little to do what the other boys did. He was happy playing with his toys and staying close to Mamma while she was at the sewing machine patching clothes or trying to write a letter to Daddy.

On rainy days we liked to play in the old barn that was only a few feet from the back door. The renters before us had donkeys and the barn was where they were kept. It still had the smell of them and so we called that place "the nasty barn." The nasty barn had a tin roof. Playing make believe in there on a rainy day was one of the most exciting things we did. We made believe that we were out on the sea in a large fishing boat in the middle of a terrible storm. Exactly how we played that out I don't remember. All I can recall is the shouting to each other because the rain hitting the roof was so loud. It was especially thrilling if lightening and thunder was a part of it. Another thing that we did in the nasty barn was to hold funeral services for dead birds and gophers. The only Bible scripture that we had memorized was John 3:16. Whoever was the minister recited the verse a couple of times and said A-Men. The rest of us sang "Jesus Loves Me." The dead was wrapped in clean cloths and buried somewhere in the back yard. We knew about funerals because Mamma always took us to church to pay our last respects when a member of the church or community passed away. I think that because we participated in every day things as very young children, a funeral did not seem like a horrifying experience. She probably had no choice. She took us with her wherever she went until we were old enough to be trusted to keep out of mischief.

The boys loved to drown out gophers from their holes. There was a large empty lot kitty corner from our yard where gophers lived in great abundance. The garden hose wouldn't reach that far so they carried bucket after bucket of water to pour down a gopher hole. Finally a half drowned gopher would crawl out and be captured by one of the boys. The little varmint was so cute, that they wanted to revive it and make it a pet. They hurried home to find rags to wrap it in, put it in a cheese box or a strawberry basket and then set it all in the warming oven above the cooking surface of the coal and wood range in the kitchen. As boys will do, they forgot about their half dead gopher and went off to play. Mamma put her foot down on any more of this kind of summer fun when the gopher came to life and fell out of the warming oven and landed on the hot stove.

The boys spent hours in make believe games and activities of their own making. Street games like kick-the-can and other hide and seek games were things they never tired of playing. The vacant lots on the south end of the block just north of 10th Street, between Main and Griffith Streets, became their playground and at least three of the families of neighborhood kids lived within sight or calling distance of the area. They laid out a ball diamond where they could safely play without breaking anyone's windows and they were small enough that they couldn't hit a ball that would go out of the lot where they were playing. This is the same lot where the boys would drown out gophers. There were many holes there!

Our Great-Aunt Marie Johnson, Grandpa Ecklund's sister, lived on the east side of Main Street in the ten hundred block and she could look down the hill on our "ball diamond." She was house bound and often bed ridden. She liked to sew and made baseball caps for all of the boys in the neighborhood, with each one's initials cut out of felt and stitched to the front of each cap. Sitting by her bed side, Aunt Marie taught me and Wanda Johnson, who was her granddaughter through marriage, to embroider. We started out by learning to do cross-stitch. How devoted she was to us even when she couldn't take care of herself. I didn't understand, as a child, but now I know that we gave her joy by just being there with her and wanting to learn from her. When I was about nine years old, Mamma taught me to make "Quick Coffee Cake" so that I could proudly take something to Aunt Marie. She liked it so much that she would even ask me to make it when she would get a taste for it. Before she became bed ridden she used to take Wanda and me into her garden to pick flowers.

Wanda Johnson – Aunt Marie – Jean 1938

One summer day as Johnny played baseball with his brothers and some neighborhood kids in their vacant lot turned baseball diamond, his foot went into a gopher hole as he was running bases. He fell and as a result, he broke his left elbow. He suffered a lot of pain physically and emotionally from that fall. It was not set properly and as a result it had to be re-broken and re-set. Physical Therapy for Johnny was carrying a lard bucket full of rocks every where he went. That was P T of the 30's! We've come a long way. It was supposed to straighten his arm after being in a cast. It only partially worked but it made him the object of mean spirited teasing. I remember that we were supposed to remind him if we saw him going without the bucket; even allowed to tell Mamma if he didn't carry it. That was like having authority to be a tattle tale now that I think about it. That simply was not right. He reacted to all of this with anger and that resulted in difficult times for him and our family. The teasing by older kids and the anger he felt toward those of us who kept him under surveillance was not checked and spilled over into his teen age years. I wish that we, as a family had understood what was happening. I feel such a sadness now. I want to remember other things.

Toys were often just things that the boys made themselves of things that they found. A rim from a small buggy wheel made a hoop to push with a forked stick and they would race them with each other. Old tires made good toys to push around or take up to the top of one of the many mine dumps to roll off and see how high they would bounce as they hit big rocks at the foot of the dump or just to see how far they would go if they happened to stay in the street and not hit anyone's fence.

Frankie was always small for his age and some of the older boys would talk him into getting inside of a big truck tire while they rolled it down the sidewalk. They had done this several times and he didn't seem to mind the ride but one day they took the tire to the top of the Capital Prize Mine dump, straight uphill from the corner of 10th and Main Streets, and convinced him that it was safe to get inside the tire. They pushed the tire off of the dump, aiming it down 10th Street. The tire didn't bounce off of any big rocks, so he was still inside when it veered off the street and crossed the vacant lots where the boys played.

Mrs. Butler was an Irish widow who lived in the house at the corner of 10th and Griffith Streets, just west of the vacant lots. When the tire had crossed the lots and the street, it slammed into her picket fence and fell flat, right there outside of her yard. Frankie couldn't get out of the tire by himself so he had to wait for those boys who pushed the tire to come and rescue him. But when they saw Mrs. Butler come out of her house waving her broom and accusing them of trying to destroy her fence, they were afraid to come near the tire to help Frankie out. After a few minutes, with Mrs. Butler standing beside the tire (she couldn't see that someone was inside of it), Frankie said, in a rather weak voice, "Somebody help me get out of here." When Mrs. Butler heard talking coming from the tire, she threw her broom up in the air and went running into her house screaming – in her very Irish accent "THE VERY DEVIL IS INSIDE THAT THING."

CHAPTER SEVEN

Daddy

IN JUNE OF 1934, Daddy had been away for over a year working for the U.S. Forest Service with the CCC. At this time he was home to visit but had some important business to take care of. He had left his tools at the Sunburst Mine almost five years prior and needed to come home and get them. Daddy drove to Silver Plume in his car, rented a team of horses and a wagon from Buckley Brothers Livery business. He drove the team and wagon to Georgetown, and picked up Billy, 6 and Frankie, 5 and the lunch that Mamma had packed. They went over Empire Pass, up Bard Creek and then to the Sunburst Mine. Daddy's tools were still there. Billy told me that he remembers sitting outside of the cabin to eat the prepared lunch, Daddy putting the tools in the wagon and heading for home. He also remembered something that made him laugh as he told it to me. He said, "Frankie and I went to the front of the wagon when we saw the horses tails begin to arch. We knew that the horses were about to poop. There was no way we were going to miss this." Daddy's back was turned to them as he sat in the seat of the wagon with the reins in his hands, but he became aware of what was entertaining them and yelled – "Get to the back and sit down – right now!" They did as they were told, but I can picture that scene: two little boys, huddled together with their hands over their mouths to stifle their laughter. Frankie told me that the horses got very tired because the trail was an extremely steep climb. He said that he saw one of the horses sit down on his haunches like a dog sits and that the horse was sitting on an ant hill. He hollered to Daddy, "Hey, the horse is sitting on an ant hill." Daddy replied, "It's all right, he will lose them when he gets up." Funny why a thing like that came to mind at his young age. Perhaps he had ants crawl on him once when he mistakenly sat on an ant hill and he remembered the discomfort. Frankie was always a lover of horses and he was feeling compassion for this big animal.

Ethel at the Sunburst Mine 1925

Because of being away from his family for such long periods at a time, Daddy longed to see us, and so his evenings in camp, when his days work with his crew was over, he thought of us until I think his heart was breaking. I sensed this from the letters that he wrote to Mamma and to us, that we came across after they had both passed away. To fill those lonely nights he wrote long letters and drew pictures for us depicting what he and the CCC boys were doing at camp. He was a remarkable artist of detail.

Bill at the Sunburst Mine 1925

In 1935, he began making up stories for us kids. He was a natural storyteller and he would write them just for us and about us. Almost always there would be a cliff hanger ending and we couldn't wait for the next letter with a story to arrive at the Post Office. The excitement of Mamma's return from her walk to the Post Office to get the mail is still exciting to me as I think about it. "Oh Mamma, is there a letter from Daddy?" "Yes" she would reply "and it's kind of fat – I wonder why?" "Oh, I wonder what he has sent us? – Please hurry and open it," was the cry from five anxious little ones. That first fat letter would be our introduction to The Whoopenhollar Stories.

Mamma waited until bed time before we got to hear what Daddy had written. He was a man of the outdoors and so it is no wonder that his creative mind spun tales of a mountain cabin, beautiful forests, streams where trout was abundant and wild animals – even little critters, and birds, would make life an adventure for five little kids that he named The Whoopenhollars. In the stories, the five children had the same names as ours. Their mother stayed at home alone waiting for her brood to return to her and tell her of all the wonderful things they had seen. Like C.S. Lewis' Chronicles of Narnia and the adventures that he created of children finding themselves mingling with animals who lived in a different kind of world, so did Daddy have that wonderful gift for telling a story where the subjects were free to think for themselves and enjoy the beauty of their surroundings, even getting lost at times.

I think the stories were not just entertainment for us, but I believe that they were character building, as well. Those Whoopenhollar kids didn't often get discouraged or scared, but when they did, the oldest of them – Billy Whoopenhollar and the next oldest – Frankie knew how to show confidence and bravery in times of trouble. A gentleness and kindness about those two were the attributes that helped them take care of the younger ones and kept fear from overtaking the camp and so the younger ones – John & Jean (the twins) and little Glenn Whoopenhollar did as they were told. Here then is the first Whoopenhollar story written in 1935 by our father – W.I. Rutherford.

March 17th 1935

Dear Kids,

Once upon a time, there were five very good children and their names were Billy and Frankie, Jean and John and Glenn.

Now these children had all been going to school all winter and they had learned their lessons very good and they had helped their Mother a whole lot. Finally, summer came and the grass was green and pretty flowers were blooming and the days were long and warm. The school had closed for the year and it was vacation time for all little folks.

One day, Billy, who was the oldest, said to his Mother, "Please let all we kids go up to the Sunburst cabin. Frank and I have been there before and we know the way and we would like to stay all night." Their mother said "If you and Frank will promise to take good care of the other children I will let you go."

And so there was a lot of hurrying to get things ready for the trip. Frank ran as fast as his legs would carry him to a neighbors place and ask a boy for the use of his burro and he came back with the burro and got a packsaddle out of the shed at his own home. His mother was getting out some food and blankets for them to take along and Jean and John were packing them in boxes. Billy went up stairs and got a 22 rifle that his Dad had bought for him and pretty soon, they were all ready to go. They put the boxes on the burro and kissed their mother good by and started off to the Sunburst.

Now the road to the Sunburst is pretty steep and they had to rest often but they were in no hurry and so they picked flowers and took some pictures with their camera while the burro nibbled at the grass that grows along the road.

Finally, they came to the cabin and they were pretty tired from the long walk and it was pretty late.

They unpacked the burro and tied him where he could get a drink and eat more grass and they started to clean out the cabin that had become dusty after a long time with no one living in it. They cleaned the stove first and John cut some wood and started a fire in the stove while Jean opened up the boxes and took out the things she needed for their supper. When she had cooked their supper they were all so hungry they forgot to wash their faces. But they never had their mother there to tell them and so it was easy to forget it

When they finished their meal, they washed the dishes and made up the beds and Frank cut more wood while Billy tied the burro in a new place where he could get more grass.

Glenn was the smallest one of the five and of course, he was more tired than the rest and soon he took off his clothes and climbed in bed. The other children talked about the fun they were having and about the pictures they had taken and about the trees and streams and rocks and birds they saw until finally they too were sleepy so they crawled into their blankets.

When they woke up the sun was just coming over the hill and they wished they had gotten up earlier because they had so much to see and do that day before they went home. Jean fixed some breakfast of oatmeal and eggs and there wasn't one speck left of the things she had cooked. Frank said "We have enough food in the box for another day. I wish we could stay longer." "But we can't" said the rest. "We promised Mama we would be back this afternoon." "All right" Frank said. "But before we go let us go over the next mountain and see what is just beyond there." "O.K." John said. I would like to see just a little bit farther, wouldn't you Billy?" Well, Billy being the oldest felt that he should look out for the rest of them and so he said "I'll tell you, we'll pack up the Jack and go around by the top of the big mountain on our way home because we must be home by dark tonight."

And so that is what they did or rather, that is what they tried to do. When they got to the top of the mountain, they saw a very pretty valley down below them. A clear running stream sparkled in the sun. "That must be the stream that comes down through Silver Plume and Georgetown" said the boys. "If we follow that stream we will come right to our home." You see, all these children lived in Georgetown.

On the way down the mountain, they saw more wonderful things. A bunch of deer trotted away and stood looking at them from a safe distance and a porcupine waddled across a log like a fat pig. Chipmunks and squirrels and birds were everywhere. They found that the mountain here was not so steep and pine trees grew thick clear down to the stream. "We will take this trail down the stream until we come to our home" they all agreed and so away they hiked thinking of all the fun they were having and wondering what their mother would have for supper when they got home

But what do you think?! They kept walking and walking and it was getting late and still they didn't see any place that looked like home. They didn't see anybody's home, just trees and a trail and a stream. Billy said. "We must be following a different stream. I don't think this one goes through Georgetown, but let us go on until we find someone who knows where we are because it is too late to go back the way we came."

The sun went down and it started to grow dusk when Billy called Frank to one side and said "Frank, we are lost and Glenn is tired. We must make camp here in the trees and wait till morning." "We mustn't let Glenn know we are lost or he would be frightened," said Frank. "We will just play like we wanted to do this all the time. What do you suppose Daddy would do if he were lost out here?" "Well, let's see, "Billy said "I'm sure Daddy would not be worried. He would say: "I'll just camp here tonight and tomorrow I'll go on down stream because a little stream always flows into a bigger one and some where along the bigger one I'll come to a ranch house or a town."

And so these boys, Billy and Frank started to laugh and the rest thought it was fun to camp out with out any cabin or tent. "John", said Billy, "if you will help me cut off a lot of small spruce boughs we can make a nice soft bed while Frank is getting wood for a fire." Soon Frank had a small fire going in a safe place and Jean was getting out what was left of the food after the burro had been unpacked and tied out to grass. Glenn carried some water from the stream and set the pail beside the fire so they would have warm water to wash their hands. After they had eaten their supper they all started gathering wood because it takes a lot of wood for a camp fire. Then they sat down around the fire and the stars came out and twinkled like little bits of fire and the children wondered if their camp fire looked like a star to some one a long way off. It wasn't long until Jean and John and Glenn grew sleepy and climbed into their blankets, but Billy and Frank still sat by the fire. When they thought the others had gone to sleep, Billy said"Frank, we have only enough food for a small breakfast in the morning and not a thing to make any sandwiches for lunch like we did yesterday and today. We have the rifle with us and we must watch very closely for a rabbit or a grouse." "That's right" said Frank. "I wish we had some fish hooks because I saw some fish in this stream, but we didn't know when we started that we would be where we could catch fish." "Gee! I'm awfully sorry that I wanted to see what was on this side of the mountain. I wonder what Mama is doing now. I'll bet she is awfully worried about us. If we only had some way of letting her know that we are all right. I'm sure we will be home tomorrow though, and she will be so glad to see us." "And what if we don't get home tomorrow," said Billy. "It is just up to we older boys to see that we can find enough for us all to eat until we come to a town. I don't think we had better go back the way we came because I'm not sure we could find the way. But it won't help any to sit here and wish we were home. The best thing to do is to go to bed and get some sleep if we are to walk far tomorrow."

When the sun shone down on their tiny camp the next morning, all the children felt much better after a good sleep in the fresh air. Soon a breakfast fire was crackling and Jean as usual went to the food box and out scampered four chipmunks. "Oh, aren't they cute?" she said. John looked up from his work of rolling up the blankets. "Take a look at our little sack of rolled oats first and maybe they won't be so cute." Sure enough the oats for breakfast were gone – all down the stomachs of the chipmunks. "Oh well," said Jean, "they are cute and anyway we still have an orange each and enough bread to make a little toast if Frank will quit throwing wood on the fire." You know it is hard to make toast until the fire dies down to red hot coals. But Frank was thinking of something else. Going over to where Billy was putting the pack saddle on the Jack, he said, "I think we can start looking for rabbits and grouse right now 'cause I got a feeling somebody's going to get hungry. What a crazy trick to leave the oats in a paper sack instead of putting them in a tin pail." "Yes," said Billy as he drew up the saddle cinch. We will know better next time. Right now it is no use wearing a sour face, so quit looking like a rainy day in Norwood, and save half of your orange for Glenn and I will do the same. At least Glenn will have some lunch even if it is only a bite of orange."

The blankets were packed on the burro, the camp fire was put out and Billy picked up the rifle as he said "well, let's go." On and on they walked. Billy in the lead and Frank next, each watching closely for the first cottontail that would mean food for them.

Glenn grew tired and they put him up on the Jack behind the blanket roll and there he rode holding on to the pack ropes. It was late in the afternoon, and Jean said, "Boys, I'm hungry. When are we going to be home?" "Oh, we'll be home pretty soon sister," said Billy and he winked at Frank. "Sure" Frank said "Home is like prosperity – it's just around the corner." About that time, a rabbit scampered across the trail and stopped in a clump of bushes. "Crack!!" went the rifle in Billy's hands and the rabbit rolled over and over. "Here Frank, take the gun and see if you can find another one while John and I clean this one," said the boy Billy. "There must be more rabbits around here" and there were more too, for pretty soon Frank came back carrying a cottontail by the hind legs. "Hooray!" said John. "Let's cook our meat right now. I'm as hungry as an old wolf." "I think we had better travel on while it is day light," said the other boys. "We are all hungry but we can wait a little while longer."

So on they went and soon they came to an old log cabin that was so old that the roof was almost all fallen in. Here they stopped to look around. The cabin was like lots of old cabins in the mountains. It was dirty and the rats had been everywhere. An old worn out pair of boots were in one corner and the old broken legged stove was covered with sticks the rats had brought in. Up on a shelf were some old coffee cans. John knocked these off with a stick. When they hit the floor the lid came off of one and out rolled some matches and buttons and string and the stub of a pencil and other little things that a man might leave in a can at his cabin.

"Well anyway we can use some more matches," said Billy as he stuck them in his pocket. "And this string too maybe," said John, picking it up. "Ouch What's that? A needle!" No, it wasn't a needle but something John had wanted. What do you suppose? – two fish hooks!

"We might as well camp here tonight," said Billy. "John can tie his hooks to the string and do a little fishing before dark." "OK." was Frank's reply. "But lets camp out, it would take all day to clean out that cabin and then the rats wouldn't let us sleep" "But," said Jean "I thought we were going home." "We are going home," the boys remarked "but first we will eat our rabbits and have a little sleep. Then Jean remembered how hungry she was and began helping Glenn gather some sticks for a fire.

As soon as John had his fish hooks ready, he dug up a few worms with the lid of a can while the other boys took care of the Jack. "I wish I were a burro," said Frank "so that I could eat grass when I'm real hungry." Billy looked at Frank – "and have big ears and sing like they do, I suppose." he said.

When Jean had supper ready, which was simply two rabbits cooked over the fire, they all went down to the stream to call John and to see what luck he was having. And there was that boy John with a fish pole in each hand, as busy as a dozen boys. On the grassy bank behind him were four good sized fish and he had another one on a hook in the water. When he saw Glenn, he waited for him, and let him pull the fish out on the bank.

Now they had some food for breakfast, thanks to John's fishing and that night they slept out again under the stars, while night birds called drowsily and a fox barked at the new moon that was just disappearing over the hills in the west.

The next morning they were on their way early; but before leaving, Billy had gone in the cabin and got the stub of pencil and finding an old piece of paper he wrote on it "We are lost. If anyone finds this, look for us down stream." And then he signed his name.

I forgot what their last names were, but I think it was "Whoopenholler." Yes, I'm sure that was his name, Billy Whoopenholler. So Billy stuck the paper in a crack on the door and picking up his rifle which he had learned was a fine thing to have, he soon caught up with the rest of the children.

By mid afternoon the two older boys were really worried. They had seen nothing to shoot that they could eat and walking so far had made them all very tired. But they knew they must keep on trying, and keep on going. The "Whoopenhollers" never gave up and these children were real Whoopenhollers, from the first "Whoop" to the last "Holler," too when they came around a bend in the trail and what do you think they saw? Why, a whole bunch of tents, great big tents, all in rows, and a lot of men, too. "Gee!" said Billy. "It's a C.C.C. camp, just like the camp at Waunita Hot Springs. Maybe they can tell us where Daddy is." And they all ran as fast as their tired legs would go. But as they ran, a man came to meet them and it was their own Daddy. My! he was glad to see them and right away he called up their dear Mama on the phone and told her the children were all safe, and that they would stay a while with him before they came home. Then you should have heard Mama Whoopenholler.!

Well Good By Kids. I hope you are all well and that you are having lots of fun. Take good care of yourselves. Love from your Dad

CHAPTER EIGHT

Mamma

THE WONDERMENT OF Daddy's make believe just filled us with desires to really and truly be what we were in the story. Oh, if only we could go off by ourselves and do all of those things – wouldn't everyone think we were the bravest and best kids that anyone in Georgetown had ever known?! "I'm glad that it had such a happy ending," Mamma said, as she tucked us in.

Going from the boy's big bedroom which had two double beds and crossing the hall into my bedroom she took her place in the hallway. This was her station every night where she met God for prayer. It was the perfect place because her voice could be heard by all five of us as we lay in our beds and she was able to keep from getting chilled as she stood with her back to the wall. This is where the chimney came up from the coal stove in the dining room and through the roof of the house and outside. Her dialogue with God was always of thankful hearts for the provisions He had made for us, for keeping us all safe and asking Him to watch over us as we slept and to grant us another day to be in His care. She always asked God to watch over Daddy and to keep him in His loving care. Then the requests for blessings on Grandma and Grandpa Ecklund, Uncle Paul, Grandma Rutherford, all of our aunts in California and our two cousins there, that we had never met, for Aunt Nona and cousin Catherine in Denver who we rarely saw, for Auntie Berg and Auntie Jellison, dearest of friends, but not relatives and then Mamma would think of someone else who needed prayer and so it would go. Five little voices echoed Mamma's "In Jesus' Name – A-Men." She kissed us each good night and quietly made her way down the stairs.

If she hadn't been so tired she probably would have danced a bit of a jig and thought to herself – "Ah, at last, peace and quiet." Peace and quiet to do something she'd like to do while the house was hers alone. But that wasn't to be; there were too many tasks calling to her. There would be a kitchen to clean, some wood to bring in from the shed so she could start a fire in the morning to make breakfast, clothes to put away, clothes to mend, a letter to write to Daddy and if she wasn't too sleepy she would write a letter to Grandma Rutherford or Aunt Nina in California.

She usually stayed up until midnight trying to get it all done and didn't want to lose any of that time alone that she cherished. Her letters would have funny little squiggle lines by the words, the tell tale signs that she had dozed off for a few seconds. Finally she would give in to her tired and sleepy body and she would go to her bed. Sleep came to her quickly and took her away from the demands on her life to a place of rest and healing. Tomorrow would be another day, maybe the mail would bring her a letter from Daddy and he would remind her of how much he loved her. It was his letters that kept her spirits up when he would be gone for such long periods of time.

Another day dawns. It is only March. If only spring would come to stay, then there would be summer and somehow things seemed easier in the summer, Mamma thought to herself, as she made a fire in the kitchen stove, put on the tea kettle and made a pan of oatmeal. "I guess I'll give the kids the stewed prunes I cooked yesterday. That will be their fruit today. I'll be glad when the rhubarb is up and ready to pick – it will be a nice change since we've used up all of what I canned last summer." she thought. When she turned around, there was Billy. He surprised her – he was hungry, that's what woke him up. He was also anxious to go to school. Billy was in Second grade and Frankie was in First. "Good morning my Sweet," she said, as she gave him a hug. Then she asked him if he would please go back upstairs and wake Frankie so they would have time to get dressed and eat their breakfast. "Don't wake the little ones," she said. It's so much easier if only two of them need me at once," she thought. The twins were only four but almost five and little Glenn was only two. "How will I manage when I need to get all five of them ready in the morning?" she mused. "Oh, no sense taking on tomorrow's worries, tomorrow will have worries of its own, and somehow the worries seem to take care of themselves; well my goodness, when the twins are old enough to go to school, Billy will be entering Fourth grade and he is already such a help. Frankie will be starting Third grade. It will be all right, they are both such good boys."

Just as certain as daylight will follow night time, so did spring arrive. Living in the Rocky Mountains of Colorado at an altitude of 8519 feet, several inches of wet snow was always predicted in the spring, making March, April and May a final good-by to winter and a blessing to the earth. The five of us loved being outdoors, no matter what the weather. The routine meant getting dressed, or being dressed, depending on our ages, playing until we were soaked and cold, coming back indoors to take off the wet coats, pants, mittens and shoes and tracking in as we came.

Following that, each one of us had to be changed into dry clothes. There on drying racks, by the coal stoves would hang our wet attire. Shoes were leather, so if we hadn't put on our rubber overshoes then we learned quite early how to wad up newspaper and stuff our shoes with it. Failing to do this meant that our shoes would dry and would not fit us again. Spring was wet and beautiful but a consternation to Mamma I'm sure.

Perhaps it was such a day as this that caused an incident that will remain with me forever. I think that we had been naughty children most of the day – quarreling and tattling to Mamma until by evening she felt defeated. Five little kids had brought her to tears and with no one to share the load she wanted to run away! She told us she was leaving and went straight to the coat rack at the foot of the stairs by the front door, reached for her coat, and began to put it on. We were all standing there, looking up at her in disbelief. "Where are you going, Mamma?" We all seemed to be in chorus. "I'm going to go over to Grandma's and stay there until you can learn to be good," she said. Oh my, it was dark outside, what would we do without her? We all clung to her coat, crying and begging – "Oh, please don't go, Mamma. We will be good, we promise." We were all crying by then. She slowly hung her coat back on the rack, looked down at all of us and wanted to believe that we would change. I've often wondered what would have happened if she had truly opened that door, walked out into the night and left us there – oh, it would only have been long enough for her to walk part way up the street; well, maybe she would have gone over to her mother, for isn't that what we all need when we are tired and discouraged? I think that she very much needed our Daddy at home.

John Jean Frank Billy 1933

There was music in our home. Mamma didn't ever study music in school but she was born with an appreciation of it and she was also born with a very nice voice. She was always "on key" and nice to listen to. She and Daddy loved to sing harmony when he was home. He also had a good voice. I remember them singing Indian Love Call, a Victor Hubert piece, Beautiful Dreamer, also by Hubert and a song titled, Mexicali Rose. There were many more, I just can't think of the names just now.

When it was quiet enough in our home, Mamma liked to listen to the radio. She and Grandma listened to the Soap Operas of the day – Stella

Dallas and One Man's Family as they did the week's laundry in the old wringer washing machine. On Wednesdays, Grandma came to our house to do the ironing and that was a good time to listen to the radio programs that they liked. There was a certain night of the week that Mamma liked to listen to "The Voice of Firestone" because it featured Evelyn and her Magic Violin. It was an hour of very fine music. I should say that I appreciated music from an early age, and so did the boys. Johnny very much liked classical and semi classical music. Billy learned to play a Hawaiian Guitar. I can still remember how in awe of him we were when he learned to play "Nearer My God To Thee.

CHAPTER NINE

Making Ends Meet

BECAUSE OF THE economy, our parents had to come up with all of the ways possible for stretching the dollar. We children were constantly reminded to "Turn off the Lights." If you turned on a light – that was O.K., but when you left the room, you must turn the light off.

In the winter we didn't heat the living room because we could do our living in the kitchen and dining room. The living room was only heated for Christmas Day. The French doors between the dining room and living room were open in the summer. I liked it when the living room truly did become a 'living room.'

Stretching the dollar to put food on the table was a daily concern. Meat being the most expensive staple, Mamma, and I suppose all of the mothers, would ask the butcher for good bone with some meat still on it. Emil Anderson at Kneisel and Anderson's store and Mr. Klein at the Red and White store, quite often had what Mamma needed in their waste piles. If the bone had more than a little meat still clinging to it, then perhaps she paid a few cents for it. With vegetables from the big garden in our yard, and some barley, our Mamma could make the most nourishing and tasty soup ever – her knowledge of seasoning, adding just the right amount of a certain herb or spice was remarkable. Daddy told us that the only thing she knew how to cook when he married her was chocolate pudding. I don't know if it was because she had a sweet tooth like most Swedes, but when she planned a meal, she always decided on what to have for dessert first. The entrée was secondary – I always thought that was wonderful – just like her!

Daddy came up with an idea of how to put more meat on the table to feed his brood. He asked Uncle Paul to help the boys – Billy and Frankie to build rabbit hutches. Daddy had to rely on Uncle Paul for many things. Once, Daddy wrote in a letter to Mamma that he hoped the boys would grow up to be fine young men like her brother Paul. He was our hero. He was kind and good to everyone and took care of the everyday needs of his parents, our Grandma and Grandpa.

Homemade Rabbit Hutch

Raising rabbits would be relatively inexpensive. During the summer months they could live on grass and dandelion greens. We had to buy pellets during the winter for their food. Daddy showed the boys how to butcher them. When prepared like fried chicken, they were delicious. In many of our old pictures, the boys, particularly Glenn, always held a rabbit. They did become pets but because we were always getting more of them, for some reason, it wasn't anything that grieved us when a rabbit was killed and butchered. Billy, Frankie and John were the ones who had to do it. I think Glenn and I were protected from that sight for awhile. Eventually, Glenn grew up enough that he also learned to make packaged rabbit meat out of a cute bunny.

Some of our food was provided in a way that was Divine Providence for us and for most of the families in town. There was, of course, a price to pay by someone else, but I know that neither I nor my brothers ever thought of that. I'm sure the mothers and fathers did. Big trucks hauled peaches from the western slope every summer. Colorado peaches from over by Fruita and Grand Junction are the finest of all peaches. It's the particular climate that they have over there. They were hauled to Denver for retail and had to go through Georgetown. It was on the big hairpin curve between us and Silver Plume that many a truck lost its load. Peaches were thrown out and scattered all over the embankment. Word got out fast – somewhat like having a town crier. The message was passed down the valley like this: "Peach truck over the bank on Plume Hill – pass it on!"

We were quick to grab all the bushel baskets we had and off we'd go with our wagon to pull our bounty home. I don't ever remember wondering about what happened to the truck driver. Did he get killed? If he survived, how badly was he hurt, and what about him not being able to work when times were so difficult? – was his truck ruined? Did he have a family to support? Driving a truck to bring produce to the market place was a good job. Now what would he do? If we had concern for all of that, would we have had such a thrill in gathering the peaches? I wonder about that now.

The embankment was crawling with people busy at work. There was a race on! Who would be able to take the most? We were always able to fill three bushel baskets and even a cardboard box. The wagon would hold only one basket at a time. One of us would pull the wagon home, while another kept guard on what was still to be hauled.

Mamma and Grandma would sort the peaches. The ones that were not too badly bruised went into one basket for canning. The terribly bruised ones were for jam. Whatever was on Mamma's list of things to do had to wait because the canning and jam making had taken priority. This was surely a gift from Heaven and not to be wasted. I remember the baskets and boxes of peaches were kept in the living room with the door closed to help keep the room cool. The peaches in the best condition were the last to be taken care of. The room was pungent with the fragrance of the 'heavenly fruit.' I loved going in there. We were very rarely allowed to help ourselves to food without asking permission first, but many pounds of something edible just showing up like that made this the exception to the rule. We did learn, however, that if we ate too many we would get sick.

One of the most precious gifts that God has given us is the sense of smell. That sense can carry you off to places you have been long ago or take you to be with a person who still lives in your memory. I can stand by the bin of peaches at the grocery store or road side stand, close my eyes and remember vividly how the living room smelled after we had gathered peaches on the hill, and how wonderful the whole house smelled, particularly the kitchen, as the fruit cooked. Watching Mamma and Grandma ladle the beautiful halves into the sterile jars will always be in my memories. What a delicious dessert – home canned peaches in the middle of winter!

* * *

There were many little things that we did to make ends meet. It seems that Mamma never threw anything away, because it could be used later and that would keep her from having to use money to buy it. We saved string, rubber bands and even wrapping paper. Gift-wrap paper was carefully taken off, being careful not to tear it. It could be ironed, folded and used again. When we had the luxury of buying fresh oranges, they always came wrapped individually in orange tissue paper. It wasn't the softest paper, but it was too good to throw away, so it was folded, put in a little box on the toilet tank to be used for, what else?-toilet paper! It was a lot softer than pages out of the Montgomery Ward catalog, which we did have to use when toilet paper was not going to be something Mamma could buy that month.

Having enough hot water in the hot water tank for bath night meant keeping a good hot fire going in the kitchen stove. Mamma always had to know how much coal and wood was still in the shed so she would know if there would be enough to heat the house and do the cooking until Daddy sent her his pay. For each one of us to have our very own warm delightful bath water would be a luxury. That would be out of the question. We got to take turns being the first one to get a bath. If it wasn't your turn to be first, then it didn't matter if you were second or fifth. The first bather had to let out a little of the water when he was through and add some clean, warm water. Each one of us followed suit until all of us had bathed. It was a beautiful bath tub made of copper. The tub was used for other things, too. Because it was copper, it was a cool place in the summer. We didn't have a refrigerator, so Mamma would put a dish of Jello in a pan of cold water and put it down into the tub to set. That really sounds strange now, when I think about it.

Growing up in The Great Depression meant finding ways to put food on the table. Some of the things we did are considered "Outdoor Fun and Recreation," today. Hunting, fishing and berry picking were fun for all of us but a necessity as well.

The boys are the ones who learned to hunt. I went fishing but mostly I helped Daddy put worms on the hook and he also taught me how to kill the fish – always trout and how to clean them, as well. Uncle Paul was a good fisherman, within his limited experience of stream and small lake trout fishing in Clear Creek County, so when Daddy wasn't home and couldn't take the boys, Uncle Paul would help them rig up fishing poles and bait a hook and let them try their luck right here in town in either one of the two creeks. Uncle Paul lived with Grandma and Grandpa at the forks of Clear Creek and South Clear Creek where 10th Street once crossed both streams to its intersection with Argentine Street. At the eddy created by the juncture of the two streams was a deep, rather quiet pool that was perfect for beginners to learn to fish. The fish were not very large; Eastern Brook Trout and anything under seven inches long had to be put back. A skillet full of eight or nine inch trout was a treat to look forward to.

When Daddy could get home in the winter time, he and Uncle Paul liked to hunt cottontail rabbits around Georgetown and in the valley between Georgetown and Lawson. As soon as the boys were old enough to shoot a .22 caliber rifle, and had enough training, they got to go along. Later they were taught to shoot a .410 gauge shotgun. All four of them learned to hunt before they were ten years old and it wasn't long before they were hunting and fishing on their own. They didn't get to hunt for deer and elk until they had reached age thirteen. That was shortly after World War II had started and the Civilian Conservation Corps had disbanded.

CHAPTER TEN

Picnics, Berry Picking And Fishing

THERE WERE MANY places to go hiking and exploring, as we got a little older. A favorite was the old wagon road up South Clear Creek, past the town reservoir. That section of the original road to the Argentine Mining District was abandoned when the automobile road up the face of Leavenworth Mountain was completed. It was not too far from home and the boys found out that there were small Brook Trout to fish for in the stream and in the late summer, there were raspberries to pick. With Daddy being gone so much of the time, Uncle Paul, who loved to hike and fish, would take the boys before they were old enough to go by themselves. He taught them how to put a worm on a hook and how to go about catching fish. He was, without a doubt, the best uncle any kid could have, especially if your Daddy wasn't around to do those things with you, even teaching you.

My, how we did look forward to the times in the summer when Daddy would be home. He had the only car that we owned with him at the CCC camp so we couldn't go anyplace very far if we didn't have him to take us. That is when we would be assured of picnics, berry picking and fishing in places too far for children our age to walk. We would pile into the '29 Whippet; Daddy at the wheel and off we'd go, heading south out of town on the road that went to the Public Service Dam. We always referred to it as "The Lake Road." Farther on is Green Lake, Clear Lake and Naylor Lake. The road ended at Naylor Lake. There also was a road from the town of Grant that went to Duck Lake. Duck Lake is south of the ridge from Naylor Lake. The two roads were connected in 1953 and became what is now Guanella Pass. It is a very scenic drive from Georgetown to Grant.

Picnic above Georgetown 1937

Fishing was at Clear Lake or at the Beaver Ponds – that's where Cabin Creek Hydroelectric generating plant is now. No more fishing at the Beaver Ponds; not since before the early 1960's. We could always find a nice place that would be level and grassy where we'd spread out our picnic cloth to put out the good lunch Mamma had packed for us. We always carried along a couple of old blankets for sitting.

Berry picking was in various places, depending on the berries we were looking for. The chokecherries were plentiful in the bushes by Mrs. Kneisel's house just south of the Capital Prize Mine. Black currants could be found anywhere there were old logging roads, where trees had fallen and the earth disturbed. They were Daddy's favorite and were best found by going west of Empire to the foot of Berthoud Pass; this is where you go to Henderson Mine now. There used to be an old sawmill there, on the road to Jones Pass. We had to climb over fallen logs and do a lot of bending over or get on our knees to pick them.

I remember a time when Johnny and I were six years old, so that would have been in 1936 that we were in that area picking berries when we had to cross a small stream. Daddy picked us up in his strong arms and one by one transported us to the other side. We didn't have long enough legs to jump over it and he didn't want us to get our shoes wet. After all five of us were on one side of the stream and Mamma still on the other, Daddy went across to get her. He picked her up, just like she was one of us and headed out into the stream. When he got midway he said "Kids, should I drop her now?" Oh, goodness, you should have heard the cries of protest! We were old enough to know that he was teasing and just having fun with us – well, I wonder about Glenn. What did he think? I must ask him when I see him. I wonder if he remembers it?

Another time when we were in that same area, probably berry picking, or it could have been that we were fishing, we did get our shoes wet. We had to take them off, hang our socks on tree branches until they dried. Then I guess we had to put on our wet shoes before we could go any farther. The memory of it remains with me because Daddy took a picture of Mamma and her five little ducklings sitting on a log with bare feet. The picture is kind of well known now. It has been enlarged to a poster size, framed in old weathered boards and has been show cased in Buff and Mary Lou's living room for some time.

Raspberries were always found along streams and open sunny areas, also around mine dumps. They were my favorite. They were so sweet that we kids ate as many as we put in our buckets – unless the folks saw us doing a little too much of that. Mamma would remind us, "If you eat too many we won't have any nice raspberry jam come winter." We hadn't learned any lessons from the squirrels – like preparing for winter. We were always hungry, that was our problem. How could we possibly think about winter when there, for the taking, was something so delicious to pop in our mouths? Somehow, it all worked out. Treats for a summer day and still we had jam for our bread in winter.

There used to be a lot of huckleberries but you don't find them anymore. Grandpa had a comb/rake for picking them because at high altitude they

Waiting for the Socks to Dry – Jones Pass – 1937

were very small but plentiful as raspberries. The comb, sometimes called a rake was very practical. It was a scoop with long tines, six to eight inches long that reached out at the bottom of the scoop. When the tines were pushed through the huckleberry bush, the berries would roll back into the scoop. It was much faster than picking each berry individually.

The fishing and berry picking were important to our family for two reasons – a family outing and the need for fruit for pies and jelly. "A treat that can't be beat" was a fresh black currant pie from Mamma's oven. It was, without a doubt, Daddy's favorite dessert. Mamma canned several pints of currants so that we could have that special treat during the winter, especially for Thanksgiving and Christmas. She was an excellent pie maker. Her crust was so tender and flaky. Before the currants were cooked for canning, enough for a couple of fresh currant pies had to be saved. Daddy's favorite of the favorite was when the pie was made from fresh currants. The praise and thanks he gave Mamma was for her, like winning a Blue Ribbon, an A Plus and the Gold Cup all at once!

Picking berries was something that Grandma and Grandpa Ecklund enjoyed from their youth. It was a sweet Swede thing to do. Mamma and Uncle Paul went berry picking when they were children, probably in the same places that I have recalled. That would be why we knew where to go, I expect.

CHAPTER ELEVEN

More Summer Memories And An Addition To Our Family

ACROSS THE STREET from our house, on the corner, is where my best childhood friend lived. Her name was Geneva Frank. We played dolls and hop-scotch. There was no lawn in her front yard, just dirt, so we scraped a hop-scotch pattern in the dirt. We would playhouse with our dolls upstairs in her bedroom, which faced the street and my house, or we would play hop-scotch for an entire afternoon.

Johnny and I had a game we liked to play and the Frank family helped us with the game. We took turns pulling each other in the wagon. The one riding was blind-folded by the one pulling. The one pulling could go where ever he/she chose, but had to stay in our own neighborhood. The one riding blind-folded had to guess where we were.

One day, the Franks saw us playing our game. Johnny was pulling and I was riding blindfolded. Mrs. Frank made a motion to Johnny to come to their porch. She put her finger up to her lips to indicate "don't talk." She and Mr. Frank lifted the wagon with me in it, up and onto the porch. Johnny pulled me right into their living room. "Where are you?"

he asked. I had not a clue and had to give up. "Take off your blind-fold," he said. I did and was I surprised! Mr. & Mrs. Frank, Geneva and her brother Norman, were all a part of our game and they were all laughing, but I think that Johnny and I laughed the loudest.

The Frank family was very good to me. Sometimes when they went to Denver to shop at the big Montgomery Ward store on South Broadway, they would take me with them. One time they even bought me a new pair of summer sandals just like the ones they had bought for Geneva. They were so cute – each strap across the foot was a different color. I'll never forget that act of kindness. It made me so happy. Mrs. Frank and Mamma always called each other Mrs. Frank and Mrs. Rutherford. I wonder why they didn't call each other Marie and Ethel? They used to cut each other's hair and give home permanents. Geneva was a year older than I. They moved away to Boulder, before either of us had entered High School.

I'm looking now to the back yard where we lived and I am sad to see that the big cottonwood tree that was not far from the back porch is gone. In that tree was a rope swing, tied to one big strong branch. It had a nice thick board for a seat. I think that it was a place for me to go to be alone and forget about chores. I made a new friend just recently, here in Arizona where I live. She has authored a children's book titled "Ted Bear's Magic Swing." Her name is Dianne Baker. Our friendship was formed when I met her for the first time and learned that she was well acquainted with Georgetown, and in our excited conversation, I discovered that she was also well acquainted with the interior of the Presbyterian Manse, having gone there several times for quiet moments of meditation when she was living in Denver. She gave me a copy of her book, inscribed and autographed.

As soon as I read it, I could feel what Ted Bear felt. He too, had many chores but they were in the woods where he lived, so he put up a swing where he could swing – up and down, back and forth, high and low and high again! (That's a quote from her book.) When he was swinging he didn't think about his chores, he would just swing. I don't remember if the boys liked to swing, all I know is that when I wanted to be alone, the swing was always available. Ted Bear taught his woodland friends that they needed to swing also and then life didn't seem so difficult – chores became easier. I wish I had told Mamma the good of swinging. I think it would have helped her with all of her chores. We could have had such fun, taking turns in the swing!

* * *

As I think about things we did in the summer, it brings to mind how we celebrated the 4th of July. In the early years of the 1930s we always had a picnic in Aunt Marie and Uncle Charles' yard. The only food items that I can remember are potato salad and watermelon. People didn't cook meat over a charcoal grill back in those days and there wasn't a fire pit for roasting wieners in anyone's yard. We only did that when we were out of town at a picnic ground or off in the woods some place. I believe that we did have wieners, but they were boiled in a pan on the stove in Aunt Marie's kitchen and brought outdoors.

We would stay all day, playing in her yard. The grown ups sat and visited. When it finally got dark enough to see the fire works, Clyde Tupes was always in charge of lighting them. Clyde was cousin Ruby's husband. It was always a large gathering for the picnic and the fireworks. Besides our family and Grandma, Grandpa and Uncle Paul, there would be Aunt Marie and Uncle Charles, of course, and Ernest and Connie Johnson and all their kids, Ruby, Clyde and Norris, and Auntie Berg and Helen After Uncle Charles died and Aunt Marie wasn't as well, we started having the celebration in Johnson's yard. By then Billy and Frankie were old enough to find easy jobs for earning some spending money. They wanted to do that so they could buy fire works! They could earn a nickel or a dime from the elderly widow ladies just for running a few errands for them. The boys weren't very old when they got jobs to carry out ashes from the coal and wood stoves in the Court House and bring in the coal and wood for the next day's heating of the rooms. They did the same kind of chores for the widow ladies, too. They didn't spend the money as they earned it, because they were saving for the 4th!! When Johnny and Glenn were old enough, they earned spending money doing the same kind of work.

* * *

In the summer of 1938, Buster came to live with us. Buster was a brown and white shepherd type dog. He was just a puppy when we got him. We traded a rabbit to the Allison kids for him. Mamma loved him at first sight. She called him "Ella Dog," as she laughed and said, "He has feet as big as an elephant." Daddy was not at home that day that we got Buster. I'm afraid we did it without asking him. Mamma had a dog when she was a child and thought it to be a good thing. Five children and one puppy, soon to be a real dog, was once again – a good thing! It was good except for the time that he chewed the back of Daddy's dress oxfords when they were sitting on the stairs to be taken up and put away. That did not go over so well, so that was not a good thing. Mamma and the five of us loved Buster with a capital L, but Daddy only tolerated him. He always felt that a dog needed to be a worker in the family. He didn't feel the need for a pet.

Buster

Perhaps Daddy thought Buster was one more mouth to feed in hard times. Mamma knew how to take care of that little problem. She would ask Mr. Klein or Mr. Anderson if they had any bones in the scrap pile after butchering. Both of these store keepers were so good to us. Yes, there was always a bone or two, and sometimes a little meat still clinging. All she needed after that were some vegetables from the garden. The soup she made was good; the same kind that she made for us, but there was one more ingredient to add, that would make it become "Dog Food." In would go some corn meal to thicken the soup. She made quite a big kettle of it about once a week. There were very rarely any scraps from our dinner plates, but if so, Buster would get that, as well.

Bill told me a story once about Buster that I think perhaps only he remembers. He said that the Katzenmeyers, who lived behind us on Griffith Street had a dog named Nicky. He was reddish brown in color, wiry haired with a sharp face and had lost his right front foot in a trap. Nicky and Buster were best buddies. Up the street lived Rocky, a big black dog. Buster and Nicky liked to tease him. They would go out into the street, put their heads together and stand like that. A big bush grew at the edge of the street near our house and Buster would hide behind the bush. Next in order of their plan, Nicky would go up the street to antagonize Rocky into chasing him. Down the street they would come, as fast as Nicky could run on three legs. Rocky caught up to Nicky about the time they reached the bush. Buster would leap out from his hiding place and nail Rocky as he went by. They rolled over and over in the dusty street, with Buster snarling and growling. The fight never lasted long. Rocky gave up quickly and ran home screeching, his tail between his legs. Buster and Nicky stood out in the street bumping heads, wagging tails, obviously giving high fives. They could always count on Rocky!

As I think about dogs, and particularly dogs growing up in Georgetown in that era and before, I don't recall that there were "breeds" of dogs as we know them now. They were just "dogs." They were such a mix that they were identified only as Bill described these three dogs to me. They were recognized by color, length of hair, size and facial features. There were no leash laws. They and all of their canine friends were free to roam around the town, congregate and socialize; free to follow their nature. Some would get hurt and sometimes a viral disease called distemper would take some down. They weren't often taken to a veterinarian for their injuries or distemper vaccinations. Buster survived all of these things, but he did have several confrontations with porcupines. He always seemed to get them in his snout. The boys took the quills out themselves with pliers. Buster was so good about it. He lived to be twelve years old, living on home-made dog food and never went to a doctor.

The reason Nicky had only three good legs was because he lost a foot in a coyote trap. His family had to care for him without a doctor to advise or administer stitches and medication. It was again, a sign of the times.

CHAPTER TWELVE

The Dangers We Faced

ONE OF THE dangers Mamma and Grandma warned us about was the occasional hobo or "tramp" as they were referred to. They were always men and would arrive on the train from Denver, knowing that the train didn't go any farther than to Silver Plume. They were just looking for a new place to stay for a few days and would go from house to house begging for a meal. They would stash their few belongings and their bed roll in an empty box car that they knew wouldn't be moved for several days, then walk up town looking for a handout. I'm sure most of them were harmless and they would often ask if there was any work they could do to pay for a meal. One of the jobs that was usually available was chopping fire wood.

They didn't go into the stores or shops and wouldn't hang around in the business district. Mamma told us not to talk to them and certainly not to go with them any where. Onetime after Mamma had fed a tramp and he had gone on his way, she found an X marked in chalk on the gate post. When Frankie saw it, he asked "Who put that X on the gatepost, Mamma?" She explained "There was a tramp here when you were in school today. I gave him an egg sandwich and a cup of coffee because he was very hungry. The mark on the post is a message to another tramp who might come by. The next tramp will know that this is a friendly household."

I remember going to Aunt Marie's house on an errand for Mamma one day. I opened her front gate, skipped along on the walkway leading around the south side of the house to the back door. Just as I came around the bay window, I spotted a man sitting on the clothes line platform eating. It startled me. It scared me so badly that I turned and ran home. When I was older I realized that he wouldn't have hurt me. Aunt Marie had given him a 'handout'. Hers was also a friendly household.

In the 1930's the road over Loveland Pass was closed in the winter. The only route west of Clear Creek County was to go over Berthoud Pass. In the summer time, Gypsy families would pass through Georgetown, usually coming from the west over Loveland Pass. They would camp right in town on the west side of Clear Creek where the little footbridge crosses at 9th Street. There were no buildings between the creek and Argentine Street, so the grass in the vacant lots made a good campsite and grazing for their horses. They took their drinking water from the creek. Probably not more than two or three families would travel together in three or four wagons pulled by big work horses. The wagons were canvas covered, well made and sturdy, painted in bright colors with lots of scroll work and painted flowers. Of course, a lot of their belongings, like pots and pans and tools hung from the sides of the wagons. The shopkeepers in town spread the word as soon as they heard that a gypsy troop had arrived, because the Gypsies had a practice of coming into a store in groups of six or more people. While some were engaging the owner or clerk, others (usually children) would be shoplifting and stuffing their pockets and loose fitting clothes with merchandise. We were always warned to stay away from the Gypsy camp, and never to talk to them. Our parents and other adults told us stories of how Gypsies would steal children from the towns where they stopped. How could a group of people traveling by horse and wagon, in a narrow valley with only one road in and out, be a threat to people who were, by this time, driving automobiles? I wonder if the adults had thought of that. Well, it served to scare us, which would tend to make us listen to our elders!

When we were kids the train was still running between Georgetown and Silver Plume and the high bridge was a big attraction for boys looking for adventure. I never would have tried doing the things they did. Frankie walked across it many times with his friends. Usually one or two of the older neighborhood boys would take him and probably Billy. I don't know if Johnny ever went. Mamma and Daddy would definitely not have approved if they had known what they were up to. Faithful dog Buster, and other kids dogs always went with them, everywhere they went and the high bridge was no exception. Buster was the only dog that would follow. If one of his masters was going across, then for sure he was going to go as well. He would carefully step from cross-tie to cross-tie. There was no walk way for foot traffic across the bridge

Georgetown Loop Railroad Bridge

When we played in our yard we could hear the narrow gauge engine taking on water and building up a head of steam after backing out of the Georgetown Station. When the boys in our neighborhood knew the train would soon be passing under the trestle at the Capital Prize Mine, they would run up and stand in the middle of the trestle to be able to look at the train as it passed under them. It was actually a game of "Chicken" to see who was brave (or stupid) enough to stay there in spite of the thick black smoke belching out of the smoke stack. I'll bet the mothers hated the black soot on the boy's faces and in their clothes. The only thing I was brave enough to do when we still had the train was to run a block north, cross the ball diamond and run up the hill when I heard the train coming – just so I could wave to the engineer! I got the idea from Mamma because she told me that when she was a little girl she used to run DOWN from where she lived in a little house on Griffith Mountain so that she could wave to the engineer. The first time I did it I hurried home to tell her that the engineer waved back to me. She smiled and said, "I'm glad honey, because he used to wave to me, too."

Ecklund Family and Buddy 1922

I don't remember how old Johnny and I were – about seven or eight, I think, when we had a terrible thing happen to us. Mamma gave us permission to go with our friend Lillian, and her little sister, June to take their family cow to graze over by Grandma's house. Mamma expected us to obey the rules about the creek, but we didn't. We got tired of watching the cow graze so we walked to the creek bank, got on our hands and knees and watched the water tumbling over rocks and rushing toward the place where it joins up with the other creek. Little June, probably about three years old, got dizzy and fell into the swift water. Lillian screamed and ran to jump in to try to grab her. She jumped in right where the two creeks come together. Oh, it hurts me to think about it. I can still see Lillian up to her waist and waving her arms above her head, screaming and crying. Johnny and I were too afraid to jump in to try to save Lillian. We just stood on the bank, scared to death! I don't know how Lillian got out of that water, but she did. We ran home to tell everybody. Little June's body wasn't found until afternoon below town near where the train took on water. It was such a horrible experience that the rest of it has been blocked from my memory.

CHAPTER THIRTEEN

Learning To Be Responsible

SUMMER VACATION FROM school seemed to last such a long time; the days just went on forever and everyone of them was filled with trying new things, learning to do more and more on our own as we ventured out of the yard, yet staying in our own part of town. Mamma had to tether us to the clothes lines when we were very little because we would have gone out of our yard and wandered off. We needed to be out in the fresh air and sunshine, so the clothes line plan worked for her.

As I continue to linger here in front of the house we called home, it seems that there is no end to what I am able to remember. I realize now what a gift God gave us that we should recall so much of the precious time we spent here. Not so long ago, Buff (Frankie) shared with me some memories he had. Being younger than he, and the only girl, I didn't know what the boys were doing, especially he and Bill (Billy). As John, (Johnny) got older he also was out and about. Glenn and I would be the last ones to gain freedom.

It seems that the boys' freedom from our own yard came gradually as Mamma trusted them to pay attention to her instructions and warnings, and felt comfortable to send them on errands. We didn't have a telephone and neither did Grandpa and Grandma, so the first "by ourselves" errands were only a block away, to take a message to Grandma and return with an answer.

The two grocery stores, Kneisel & Anderson and A.G. Klein's Red and White Store delivered groceries every day. Buff said, when he was sharing memories with me, "Mamma would send us uptown with a list of things she needed and we would leave the list at one of the stores. If it was a small list or she needed something from the Drug Store, we would take our little coaster wagon and carry back what she needed. When we were younger than about seven years, she didn't expect us to carry anything home from the stores because older kids would stop us and sometimes take things away from us. Two or three of us would go together and Billy, being the oldest, often ended up defending me and Johnny against would-be bullies", he said.

Being older, and having the Katzenmeyer, Johnson and Rockwell kids to play with, meant that often times the boys would go off with them to broaden their world. Finding new places and things to do was exciting! Often Mamma didn't know where they were or what they were up to. In the late 1930's, they were old enough that she trusted them to stay out of trouble and hopefully out of danger. However, they took some pretty risky chances that Mamma DID NOT know about. After all, their Daddy had made an impression on them that they could do remarkable things and could be trusted to be on their own as Whoopenholler boys. Well, then, surely the Rutherford boys would be able to do likewise. How were they to know where the Whoopenholler in them left off and the Rutherford began? They had rules to go by and both of our parents reminded us again and again about the consequences of going beyond our boundaries and breaking the rules. There were definite places where we could not go. In the spring, when the two creeks were running fast and the banks full, we knew that to play along the creek was out of bounds. We were also warned about the dangers of going in old mine portals and that was strictly forbidden.

One of the self-discovered play grounds for the boys was the train yard at the railroad depot. There were always empty coal cars or box cars waiting on the sidings with access to the brakeman's walk-way, up high along the top. The boys would scamper up and down the ladders pretending to be train robbers.

Jean and Frank with Dutch
and Leonard Katzenmeyer and Nicky – 1938

CHAPTER FOURTEEN

Vegetables and Celebrations

"JUST AS SOON as school is out, I want you to come straight home," Mamma said, as we left for school, "We have to get the rest of the vegetables dug before we get a frost, which could be any night now that October is here."

I don't know how the boys liked doing it. I don't think we ever talked about it. I liked to do it because it was a change from doing house work, and we all got to work together. We had to work fast because the sun was gone from the floor of the valley by three o'clock in the afternoon in the fall of the year. After the sun went down, the temperature fell quickly.

"Billy, you open the cellar door, go down and get the bushel baskets and Frankie, you can help carry them out to the garden," Mamma said as she got things organized. Billy liked being asked to do things that started a process because he was the oldest and the strongest. Opening the cellar door meant rolling the old wringer washing machine out of the large pantry, where it was kept – except on wash day. It sat smack dab on top of the cellar door. "Come on Frankie, give me a hand moving this thing and then I need you to help me with the cellar door. Hold it open while I go down. I'll toss the baskets up to you." Frankie did as he was asked and because he couldn't see down there, he asked Billy, "Do you see anything?" "What do you mean?" Billy called up in response to Frankie's question. "Well, do you see any mice, or maybe spiders?" Billy called back "No, I don't see anything, it's too dark. I'd ask you to get me a flash light, but Mamma is waiting so we'd better hurry. I can see the baskets, they are right here at the foot of the steps." "O.K.," said Frankie. "Maybe Mamma will let us look around with a flashlight when we bring the baskets back with the vegetables and put them in the cellar." "Maybe so," said Billy. "Let's ask her if we can."

"Johnny, see if you can find some gunny sacks in the coal shed," said Mamma. "I think there are some just as you go in the door, hanging on the wall to your right." Johnny had just pushed his shovel into the soft dirt when he was asked to look for the sacks. He knew what they were for. This was a job we did every year when we got big enough to help.

Here came Billy and Frankie with four bushel baskets and right behind them came Johnny with the sacks. Jean and Glenn were waiting to help, too. "Billy, when you and Frankie turn over the dirt and find the carrots, Johnny and Glenn and I will cut the tops off and shake the dirt off of the roots," said Jean. "We can save the tops to give to the rabbits, "she added. Besides carrots, there would be turnips, parsnips, rutabagas and beets. There might be a few radishes left, but not many because we loved to pick them and eat them as a snack all summer long. The other vegetables that had been growing were peas, green beans and lettuce. By the time autumn came, the above ground vegetables were gone. They had all been eaten. Billy suggested that they could take turns digging. He knew that Johnny really wanted to dig. Whether Jean and Glenn could do it, he didn't know, but they could try.

Mamma was in the house looking for old newspapers. Grandpa used to give us the Denver Post after he was through reading it. I don't think Mamma had much time to read the paper, but when Billy was about in Fourth Grade, he was an excellent reader and he would read all of the Sunday funnies to us. He would lay the paper on the floor and we would all lay down on our stomachs, chins resting in our hands, and listen to him. "Oh, here comes Mamma with lots of paper," said Glenn. "I know how to wrap the vegetables in the paper and you could put them in the gunny sacks, Jean." "O.K.," she replied.

They worked like five little beavers with their mother and they were able to dig up and pack two long rows of vegetables. It was getting pretty chilly now, and Mamma said, "That's enough for this afternoon. If we work like this tomorrow after school, we will have the job done."

We all helped to carry two of the baskets into the house. That's when Frankie said, "Mamma, can we have a flashlight when we take these baskets down the cellar steps?" "Yes, you should have one so you can see where you are going. It's terribly dark to be taking things down there. I don't want any one of you to get hurt" was her answer to his question. Billy winked at Frankie as much as to say – I knew she would say yes!

With the beam of the lamp held by Frankie, Billy went down the steps, turned around and said to Johnny, "Shove that basket close to the edge so I can get a hold on it." Johnny, trying his best to see down in the dark place below, helped Billy with the basket, then Billy said, "We can all get down here, there is enough room for all of us." Johnny didn't need any coaxing, but Jean and Glenn were a little bit afraid of the dark and dirty looking place with steep steps and were wondering what they might see in there. "Do you see anything?" "Well, sure I see some shelves with canning jars on them and I can see the walls and" – Billy's answer was cut short as Jean said, "No, I don't mean like that, I mean do you see any mice or big spiders?" Jean hated both of those things! Billy told her that all he could see about spiders were all of their webs and no mice. He said he would get rid of the webs. He wasn't afraid of anything! "You and Glenn come on down." Very cautiously, and with Frankie holding her hand, she took the steps down. It took a minute to get her eyes adjusted, then she said "Come on Glenn, I'll hold your hand." Oh, my, she was so brave now! Glenn went down then. It was a little crowded but they moved apart from one another. Frankie, still holding the flashlight, shone it around the whole cellar which wasn't more than 6' x 8'. It felt cold and damp and had a peculiar smell. There was nothing to see, it was just dirt walls and a dirt floor. The steps were made of wood. Mamma said, "Time to come up now. Leave the baskets of vegetables there and tomorrow we should have two more. When we can't go to the garden to get vegetables after winter comes, we will know where we CAN get them and they will be just as good as the day we dug them." Maybe she would even ask us to go to the cellar for her, we would like to do that. Even Jean and Glenn wouldn't mind. They got over their fear of the dark cellar that first year that they got to help. Sometimes there were too many vegetables to put in the cellar so we dug them up, wrapped them in newspaper and put them back into the ground. Newspaper is a great insulation against frost.

* * *

October was almost over and it was time for Billy's birthday on the 30th and then Halloween. We didn't have birthday parties; well we did, but it was with just our family. Mamma asked each one, when it was his birthday, what he wanted for supper. We called it supper – not dinner. She made a two layer cake, frosted it and even decorated it by writing HAPPY BIRTHDAY, followed by our name. We thought it was just wonderful and beautiful to see our name written on a cake – like having your name 'in lights', I suppose. Grandma Ecklund made ice cream and we either celebrated at our house after supper or we would take the cake to Grandma and Grandpa's house when Grandpa wasn't able to walk to our house anymore. The ice cream was different. It was some kind of powder in a box that Grandma bought at the store, mixed with milk and put in ice cube trays in the little freezer compartment of her refrigerator. When it had started to freeze a bit, then she took it out and beat it with an egg beater and put it back into the trays and then into the freezer again. We thought it was very good. As I remember it, it was kind of icy, like glace' in France. I learned that, when I lived in France, tasted glace' and I thought of Grandma's ice cream.

Grandma had a refrigerator because Uncle Paul worked for Public Service and he was able to give that nice appliance to his mom probably at an employee's discount. Our refrigerator was a bucket of ice cold water on the floor of the pantry by an open window which was on the north side of the house. That was excellent planning – building the pantry on the north side of the house – WOW. In that bucket of cold water was always the milk and Buster's pot of home made dog food. There were no left overs, so we didn't need a place to keep them from spoiling.

We had enough people in our immediate family to have a pretty big party. There would be Grandma and Grandpa, Uncle Paul, Mamma, Auntie Berg and the five of us. Even bigger and better if Daddy happened to be home. If Mamma's cousin Ruby and son Norris were in Georgetown taking care of our great Aunt Marie, then it would really be a big party. Somehow, that one cake was cut to treat every one there. I don't remember any presents to open, not when we were little. There just was not money for presents, but we didn't know the difference. We honestly did not know that people got presents on their birthdays. I remember Mamma buying presents for us in the 40's after the Depression was over.

Halloween followed Billy's birthday and it was fun. We didn't go Trick-or-Treating to the neighbor's houses as no one had money to buy candy for kids. We did get to go to the grocery stores and to the pool hall. That was the best place of all. Mr. Kirkpatrick gave every kid a big candy bar – those big 5 cent ones!

Mamma would help us carve a pumpkin and put a candle in it. We liked to set it on one of the gate posts. Once I was wearing a mask with whiskers on the chin. I climbed up on the fence, looked down into the jack-o-lantern and my whiskers caught on fire. Mamma was right there beside me, but it happened so fast that she wasn't able to stop me from bending down and looking in. I don't remember which of the boys it was, but a couple of them grabbed me off the fence, shoved me to the ground and rubbed my face into the wet grass. The fire was out and I didn't get burned. I got a lot of attention from that. The boys were heroes and Mamma was so proud of them! We never had masks with whiskers again.

* * *

I don't remember a Thanksgiving or Christmas that Daddy wasn't at home to celebrate those special holidays with us. Getting the house ready for his homecoming was always the most exciting time, but it would almost make me sick to my stomach because of the waiting. It would be after dark by the time he could reach Georgetown. He had to drive all day to come from down near Pueblo in the San Isabel National Forest where he worked in the CCC camp.

Supper was over and we had all helped to get the dishes washed and put away. I don't know what the boys were doing. All I could think about was that at any minute, Daddy could be walking in the back door. Mamma called out "Jean, where are you?" I got up from my look-out and came into the kitchen. "I'm lying at the foot of your bed looking out the window, watching for Daddy," I said. "Oh, all right dear, that's fine" she answered. I went back to my place, there at the foot of her bed. I lay watching every car that came into town. Some turned up Rose Street and when that happened, I'd just sigh. I knew that would not be Daddy. When I saw car lights come over to Taos Street, my heart would jump and I'd hold my breath to see if it would turn by our fence at the corner of Taos and 10th Streets. Sometimes it just kept going past our house, but – OH, that car is slowing down and now it is turning – how I would cry out when the lights of the car came to the place where it could turn into our yard. Sure enough, it did turn in. I jumped from the bed, ran into the kitchen and then I got to do it – make my very important announcement – DADDY IS HOME! It seemed that it took him forever to turn off the engine and the lights and make it up to the porch. We were all crammed together, trying to open the door at the same time, and that doesn't work when you have too many hands. Finally the door opened wide and there he was! We were hugging him and climbing on him 'til it was a wonder that he didn't get knocked off his feet before he ever got to hold Mamma and kiss her.

Everyone was talking at the same time. Finally he got to sit down at the table and Mamma brought a left over supper to him that she had saved in the warming oven. We all sat down and watched him eat. It was such a grand thing to watch – a grown man at our table and it was our very own Daddy. The dessert that Mamma had made and kept from us, was now being served. It had the "feel" of being a Grand Party!

Soon it was time to be off to bed, but tomorrow would be Saturday so we would get to be with him all day. We lay in our beds and could hardly sleep. We knew that he had bought each of us a treat and we knew what it was because he always brought the same thing. Some place on his way home, he had stopped and bought five boxes of Cracker Jacks. We were crazy about Cracker Jacks and it was such a treat to get them. I had a special way of eating mine. I liked to open the box, find the prize

Home for Christmas 1935

inside, and pour the caramel corn into a bowl. When that was done, I would climb up on Daddy's lap with the bowl. I wanted to share my treat with him. We had it all worked out. Each of us would put a hand in the caramel corn. My hand reached up to Daddy's mouth and his hand reached down to mine. Feeding each other is what we did. The week-end would go by far too fast. I think it must have been like a whirl-wind for Daddy, because each one of us wanted his attention.

I especially liked it when he would play house with me. I pretended that he was my husband and that I cooked his meals. I remember telling him, "You will have to wash your hands and face before you come to the table." He obliged, being a good husband. I can still see him rolling up his shirt sleeves as he pretended to splash water on his face, rub his hands together and then drying on my make-believe towel. While he was 'cleaning up' as we called it, I was fixing his supper. I served him on my doll dishes and we had to use our imaginations as to what was being dished up. You can be sure that there was meat, potatoes and gravy, for that's what a man liked for his supper. My Daddy also liked to have a cup of tea with his supper and I had a tea pot and cups and saucers. Everything was perfect. He never once indicated that he didn't like 'playing house.'

I loved him so much and he loved me the same. I liked sitting in his lap when I was little.

I'd nuzzle my face into his chest. His shirt had such a good fragrance; like pipe tobacco and fresh cut wood. Daddy had a love song that he sang to me every time he had to leave to go back to the CCC camp. The name of the song is "My Little Girl," written in 1915 by Sam M. Lewis. In his strong and very good voice, I believe it was tenor, he sang to me –

> *My little girl, you know I love you and I long for you each day.*
> *My little girl, I'm dreaming of you, though you're many miles away.*
> *I see the lane down in the wild wood where you promised to be true.*
> *My little girl you know I love you and I'm coming back to you.*

I have remembered the words and the melody to the song all of these years. Note: music and lyrics to this song are here. Thanks to David Rutherford who found it for me and added chords.

CHAPTER FIFTEEN

Thanksgiving

THANKSGIVING IS ONE holiday that I remember as always being pretty much the same. We looked forward to it because there seemed to be plenty of food every year, and it was so good. The menu was always the same and in re-living it in my mind, I am quite sure that Grandpa Ecklund must have been the person that God used so that He could provide a fine dinner for us. God did always provide and I think that he asked Grandpa to buy the turkey. Our family came up with all kinds of vegetables, and we know where they came from! We had pumpkin, mince meat and black currant pies. Mamma made her own mince from the neck meat of venison. She canned it, and a large part of the rest of the meat, as well. We had no other way of preserving food. The black currants were also canned. They were from the wonderful summer when we all went black currant picking.

Our Thanksgiving table was loaded with food for Kings and Queens! I remember that we used the nicest dishes and serving pieces that Grandma's house and ours could come up with. White table cloths and linen napkins were used and if there was any silver, it was polished. We had two tables set, one in the dining room and the table in the kitchen.

The Thanksgiving that stands out in my mind is one when someone, I don't know who, gave our family a bottle of Blackberry Wine. We never had wine, beer or whiskey in our house. If our folks had an appetite for any of those things, there certainly wasn't any money to buy it. I've always been grateful that Daddy's priorities were his family and providing for them.

The bottle of Blackberry Wine had a curiosity about it for me. I think all of the grownups thought it was a very nice gift and were looking forward to having a small glass for dinner. "What is so great about Blackberry Wine," I wondered. It had been placed in the bucket of ice cold water in the pantry. One of the grown-ups had opened it so it was no problem checking it out. I just wanted to know what in the world it tasted like.

I was asked to spell Grandma from her place at the hot stove, stirring the gravy, waiting for it to come to a boil. It takes awhile at high altitude. She would stir and then she would call me to come and stir for awhile. "Yeanie, please come and stir da gravy," she would say in her darling Swedish accent. But it was while she was stirring, that I would go to the pantry and have just a sip of the Blackberry Wine. This went on until I had had quite a few sips. At one point, when it was my turn to stir, standing over the hot stove, I must have given away the secret that I thought I was hiding. Grandma took notice of me and said to Mamma, "Ettel, I tink dat Yean has been in da vine." Oh no, was I really acting different? I was trying not to do that, because I can tell you that I did feel different. I wanted very much to just laugh. I felt as though everything was very funny. I liked the wine! I was scolded pretty severely by Mamma. I wonder now if that was because there wouldn't be enough for all the grown-ups after my imbibing.

CHAPTER SIXTEEN

Christmas

THE TRADITIONAL CHRISTMAS began the year that we moved into the manse in 1933 and continued to be celebrated the same way for many years. There would be no display of decorations before December 25th. Because there was little money for buying presents, our parents made the Christmas tree the focal point and their gift to us. We did put our stockings out on Christmas eve. Each one of us chose one from our chest of drawers and in those days we all wore long tan colored cotton ones. We looked at each others stockings, making sure that we didn't have a smaller one than some one else. Mamma must have figured out how they could all be the same size. She was always so fair about everything.

There was a great secret going on after the five of us had gone to bed. While visions of sugar plums danced in our heads, Daddy and Mamma were busy in the living room decorating the Christmas tree. Daddy had already cut the tree and it had been hidden somewhere in the back yard or in the shed. After they were finished stringing the lights and putting the decorations on the tree, they hung sheets over the French doors so that we would not be able to see in the living room when we woke up in the morning.

One Christmas Eve, after Mamma and Daddy had tucked us in bed and given us strict orders to go right to sleep, we just couldn't calm down. We had been told, of course, that Santa Claus would come and leave presents for us after we were asleep. Mamma would hear us talking and would call up to us, "You have to go to sleep, or Santa Claus won't come." Oh, we would try so hard, but sleep wouldn't come. Then we heard the front door bell ring! We became very quiet as we listened for Mamma to answer the door. "Oh, hello Santa," she said. A deep voice asked "Are the children asleep yet?" Mamma answered "No, they are not asleep Santa." "Well, I'm sorry to hear that. I won't be able to leave any presents here; I'll have to go on, as I have a lot of houses to go to tonight," Santa replied. Then we heard Mamma say "I don't want them to be disappointed, Santa. Will you please come back again before you leave Georgetown? Maybe they will be asleep by then." Santa answered "Yes, I'll come back, but you know, they will have to be asleep." "Thank you Santa, that is so good of you – good-by." Then we heard the door close and bells ringing out in the street. They sounded like the bells that are on horses that pull a sleigh. We were awestruck as we pictured Santa in a sleigh being pulled by his reindeer, for that is the way the story went that Daddy had read to us, just that evening. It was called "The Night Before Christmas." Daddy always said funny things to make us laugh. When he read the part of the story that says – Away to the window he flew like a flash, tore open the shutters and threw back the sash – He said, "tore open the shutters and threw up the hash." Sleep did finally come, as did the morning.

We were quick to get dressed, eat our breakfast, help to wash the dishes and get ready for the big surprise that was about to be revealed. As the five of us waited anxiously for Daddy to remove the sheets from the French doors, I remember that there was pushing and shoving, trying our best to get a peek, or to be the first one to see the surprise awaiting us. Oh, my, the sheet came down, Daddy opened the doors and then we saw it!

The tree sat on the big library table in the north window, lights on it aglow and reflecting on the beautiful shiny ornaments hanging from each branch. Because there was no mantel, the stockings were laid out on the divan. There were real treats in them. An orange and a bright red apple, some hard candy (we called it Christmas Candy) and some chocolate covered creme drops. We had to dig deep into the toes to get every single nut. There were filberts, walnuts, peanuts, hazelnuts, Brazil nuts, almonds and pecans! We loved getting that good fruit and the treats of candy and nuts.

I realize how blessed I was, being the only girl. I always got a doll, or maybe doll dishes or paper dolls, but I remember the boys got things that had to be shared. In 1936, I got a baby doll. Billy, Frankie and John got a Big Streak wagon and Glenn got a stuffed horse that was given the name "20 Grand." Perhaps that was the name of a famous race horse back then.

Christmas Presents 1936

I believe it was in 1935, when I was 5 years old that I found my Christmas present in the big upstairs closet. It was an eighteen inch doll. Not a baby doll, a little girl doll with real hair. I wasn't snooping, I accidentally found it. Quite often, Mamma would ask one of us to run upstairs to get something in that closet for her. That is where she stored the home made jelly and canned fruit. Possibly, I was on an errand to bring some jelly to the kitchen. I can still remember how I felt. I looked at the doll, touched her and then drew my hand back, as if I were being naughty. I was sick at heart, a real feeling of disappointment. If I had been snooping and found the doll, I would have felt ashamed, but that wasn't the case. I never did tell Mamma, but it did take away the joy when we went into the living room on that Christmas morning, for I already knew what Santa had brought for me – and I was no longer going to be able to believe in Santa Claus. I remember that I didn't want the boys to know, so I went along with the fun of believing because I really wanted to believe in Santa myself. I wonder if maybe Glenn was the only innocent one by that time. He would have been three years old. Surely Billy, age seven, knew, and had not told the rest of us.

Not so long ago Bill told a wonderful story about Grandma Ecklund's Swedish Christmas. It was a true story told from his memories. He submitted it for publication in the Colorado AAA magazine, Encompass, and it was published! That meant a lot to him and to all of us, making us proud, I might add. He waited almost a year, wondering if they were going to accept his writing, then he got the news right about the time he celebrated his 80th birthday. What a nice gift to mark a milestone. Here is the story as he wrote it and how he remembers it happening.

> Each Christmas season brings back memories of Christmas in Georgetown in the early 1930's. This was at the peak of the Great Depression, money was scarce and hard to come by, and it took some scrimping and saving to have any kind of Christmas celebration at all. My Swedish grandmother insisted upon having a traditional Swedish Christmas, complete with all the goodies associated with such an occasion.
>
> A Swedish delicatessen on West Colfax Avenue was the source of everything Grandma required. My uncle would put a dollar's worth (5 gallons) of gasoline in his Model A Ford, which was enough to make the round trip to pick up everything Grandma needed. My recollection is that the road over Floyd Hill and down Mount Vernon Canyon was unpaved gravel at that time. He would bring back the lingon berries, ingredients for sylta (head cheese), rye flour for Limpa rye bread, and most important of all, lutefisk.

Then Grandma would set about preparing everything for the repast. The lutefisk had to be soaked for several days, with daily changes of water, to get rid of the lye. (Question: Why do Swedes eat lutefisk? Because Norwegians eat it, and a Swede can do anything a Norwegian can do!) Then came all the cooking and baking, and finally the finished products to be enjoyed by all.

Yes, Christmas back then was a truly memorable time. I wonder how many Americans today have such rich traditions still part of their lives. I certainly wouldn't want to go back to the hard economic times we had in the 1930's, but I'd sure love to ride along in the Model A Ford and bring back the supplies for Grandma's Swedish Christmas once again.

I loved this story because I picture a little boy about five years old sitting at the kitchen table at his grandmother's house. She is talking to her son, asking him to write down the things she will be needing for the up coming Christmas dinner. She didn't write the list, because her spelling in English was very difficult. The grandmother spoke, the young man wrote, and the little boy listened. The list was completed.

The memory of what happened around that table was never forgotten and I think that of the three at the table, the little boy was especially blessed because he would carry it in his heart and memory for over seventy years, in spite of suffering a stroke in his seventieth year.

I wonder how long I've been here in front of the Presbyterian Manse. There must not be a Neighborhood Block Watch in Georgetown or I would have been questioned by someone passing by, as it would appear that I have been loitering and why did I constantly have my gaze on this particular house for such a long time? Apparently no one has noticed me. If someone had, and asked me what I was doing, believe me, I would ask them to sit awhile with me and I would tell them. I guess I'd better go. I don't really want to, but I must. I wish that the boys could have been with me today. I will visit with them while I am on this trip, however I won't get to see Johnny, because he can't come back to see us anymore, nor can we go to visit him, not where he is living now. I like to think that he is always looking down at all of us; he was so full of fun, loved to laugh, and always enjoyed coming back home to visit. I miss him, but I sense his presence and I can hear him laughing.

Jean and John-Summer 1933

WHOOPENHOLLAR FAIRY TALE Camp F-48-C July 7th 1935

Dear Kids –

Once upon a time the Whoopenhollar kids ate a lot of ice cream and cake for supper and soon afterward they cleaned up their playthings from the floor and began undressing for bed.

Their tummies were so full that they didn't go to sleep for quite a while but finally the sand-man came and right after that a loud knock came at the door. Mama Whoopenhollar answered the knock but it was so loud that all the kids heard it.

"Why Hello" the kids heard their mother say. "You are Little Fairy Play, aren't you? We have heard of you being around here but I haven't seen you since I was a little girl."

By this time the kids were sitting up in bed and their eyes were big and wide and they were as still as mice, listening.

"Yes, you remember me." the kids heard Fairy Play say to their mother. "I have come to take the little folks to Fairy Land for awhile. We have so many new things there since you were a little girl that I am sorry you can not go along. But you understand that only little folks can go to Fairy Land."

"Oh that is all right Fairy Play" their mother said. "I have been there and now I am glad that the children can go. I will call them."

But she didn't have to call them for they were all ready coming down the stairs just as fast as they could come. And the next instant they were standing around the funniest boy they had ever seen. He was no bigger than Billy Whoopenhollar and yet he looked just lots older. He was so full of fun that his eyes sparkled and his mouth was in the shape of a smile all the time. He couldn't change that even if he wanted to, and fairies, you know, can change most anything. This was "Fairy Play" and the kids felt that they had always known him. "Just wait till we get our clothes on" said the kids, "and we will be ready." "Ho Ho" laughed Fairy Play, "You are all ready now." And the kids looked at themselves and then at each other. They couldn't understand what had happened to them so suddenly! Billy was dressed in an Aviator's suit, Frank had a real Cow Boy suit, Johnny a Policeman uniform, and Glenn had on a little Indian suit. And then they all looked at Jean, their little sister. She looked just like the pictures of Fairy Princess! Her dress sparkled with pretty jewels and on her shoulders were fluffy butterfly wings.

They all followed Fairy Play out into the yard and there before them was the prettiest little airplane they had ever seen. "You can all take turns flying the plane, said Fairy Play and so they all took their seats while Fairy Play showed them, one at a time how to handle the plane.

Away up in the clouds they soared and out over the mountains, and as they looked down they saw the lights of town twinkle far below them.

On and on they flew until the kids saw that the night was changing to a queer day. Not the light of ordinary days, but a soft rose colored light. They all looked around for the sun that shone such a pretty light but there was none. Then they looked away down below them where the light was the brightest and there sure enough was Fairy Land, the most beautiful place they had ever seen.

"Where does all the pretty light come from?" asked the children. "It comes from the eyes and smiles and pretty faces of all the happy children," said Fairy Play.

The plane dipped down and came to a stop on the soft green grass. "Is the light any brighter because we are here?" the children ask. Fairy Play smiled until his whole face was rosy. "You can always make the world brighter when you smile," was all that he would say.

Everywhere the kids looked there were pretty play houses and flower gardens and green fields with pretty ponies grazing and children were running and playing and laughing.

The Whoopenhollar kids couldn't stand still another minute. They all joined hands and danced around Fairy Play.

When they looked up again there were a lot of other fairies around them. "These are all my helpers." said Fairy Play. "Here is Fairy Good and Fairy Joy and Fairy Fun and lots of others. Now Fairy Good would like to take you into the big palace of the Fairy people and show you all the good and wonderful things that we have here and after that Fairy Fun and Fairy Joy will show you the way they have a good time. And now, I must be going to find other little folks who haven't been to Fairy Land." So with a great big laugh he hopped into the plane and was gone.

Fairy Good proved to be a very good guide. The children went skipping with him thru (sic) all the big lovely rooms of the Fairy Palace. The first place they came to was the Fairy Kitchen. What a place it was!

Some fairies were making candy and others were making cakes and cookies and ice cream and everything that the kids liked the best.

"All the fairies take turns here and they laugh and sing while they work and so that makes them happy," explained Fairy Good. The fairies gave them all the good things they could eat and told them to come back when they wanted more.

From the kitchen they went to a great large room where they could hear the sweetest music and so on thru (sic) all the lovely rooms of the big Fairy Palace.

When they came to the outer door into the flower covered yard, Fairies Fun and Joy were waiting there with five little cars. Other little fairies were turning hand springs and making all sorts of monkey shines which made the kids laugh until they held their sides.

Then they jumped into the cars, the funny fairies jumped on behind and they went whizzing out to a big lake.

They left the little cars and got into a sail boat with pretty colored sails and painted sides. The fairy boat was so light that it tossed on the waves like a cork.

"Now, I wish I had a sailor suit instead of this Policeman's uniform," said Johnny and he had hardly spoken the words when the Policeman's uniform turned into the prettiest sailor suit he had ever seen. When Johnny looked bewildered, the fairies just laughed and laughed.

After they had ridden for awhile in the sail boat, they went back to the shore and a new Fairy was waiting for them. Fairy Fun said "this is Fairy Book – you kids have read a lot about him but I'm sure this is the first time that you have really seen him. Fairy Book will now show you the things he writes about."

Fairy Book looked lots older than the other fairies and Billy wondered how long it took him to write all the fairy stories and Mother Goose rhymes. Frank wanted to call him "Mr. Book" but he didn't know if that would be right. But Fairy Book took their hands and danced away with them without giving them any more time to wonder how old he was.

They saw so many wonderful things that they couldn't even remember all the places that Fairy Book took them. They saw the "Old Lady That Lived In The Shoe, "Little Red Riding Hood" "Little Tom Horner," "Jack The Giant Killer," "Little Bo Peep" and just about all the fairy people that Fairy Book writes about.

Then the worst thing of all happened – Glenn said, "I wish I could be home to tell Mamma all about Fairy Land." ZIP – and Fairy Land was gone!

The next thing They heard was Mamma Whoopenhollar "Are you kids ever going to get up for breakfast?" whooped Mama.

The kids hollered back: "We don't feel so good Mama."

"It must have been all that ice cream and cake you ate last night. You rolled and tossed all night long. Now come on down stairs. I won't holler at you kids anymore," she whooped.

And so the Whoopenhollar Kids finally realized they were back from Fairy Land and safe at home

Well good by kids
Yours, Daddy

WHOOPENHOLLAR STORIES

LITTLE JERRY BEAVER

Dear Kids,

Once upon a time there lived in the big beaver dam, a little beaver named Jerry.

The big beaver dam was in a large stream that came tumbling down from the mountains. The water was crystal clear and rainbow trout of all sizes were in the deep shady pools that were made by the beaver up and down the creek. There were lots of beaver dams but the one where Jerry lived was the largest of all. No one knew how long ago the first beaver had built this dam nor how many beaver still lived there.

Each year the dam grew larger and the beaver houses grew bigger as the old beaver worked hard to build the dam higher so that it would back up more water.

Jerry Beaver had a good and wise father and mother. Jerry liked to play sometimes when he was supposed to help with house building. This would make his father provoked and a few times Jerry got a good sound slap across his ears.

Jerry liked to swim across the big dam, taking a piece of tree with him in his sharp teeth. That was much easier than cutting down the tree or digging mud from the sides of the bank to use as plaster in building the dam or the house larger. But his father and mother knew that Jerry would have to learn to do all these things before he would be able to take care of himself.

A wise old beaver always cuts his trees on a steep hillside by the dam so that it will be easier to slide them into the water. After he has dragged one tree down to start a trail, he goes in and out of the water with his long fur dripping. This makes the trail slippery as he pats the mud down with his tail and soon he has a slide that will take the pieces of trees almost into the water with just a little start.

Now Jerry just loved to scoot down the slide for fun and hit with a plunk into the water just like a boy playing in a park. Jerry's father liked to see him play and besides it kept the slide nice and slick for the small logs, only Jerry hated to be told to take a log down now and then. It was so much more fun to slide down without them.

Early one morning, Jerry's father and mother climbed to the roof of their house made of mud and sticks. They often did this as it was easier to see all around from atop the house.

On this particular morning they had good reason to be watching, for up in the tree tops, a good many yards from their house, they saw smoke curling up.

"Maybe it's a forest fire" said father beaver, "and our pretty trees will burn, then what shall we do for bark to eat and with out trees to shade and hold the snow in winter, the water will come rushing down the mountain sides and wash our dams away."

"I smell something more than wood smoke," said mother beaver. "What can it be?"

"Oh Jerry," called his father, "come here this minute" Jerry came but not too quick as he disliked being called out of his warm bed so early. "Jerry," continued his father when Jerry had rubbed the sleep out of his eyes and the water out of his ears, "I want you to swim down to wise old Grandpa beaver and ask him if he has seen anything or smelled anything strange to him and remember what your Grandpa tells you so you won't make a mistake.

So away went Jerry in a hurry before his father would ask him to take a log down to Grandpa on his way there.

"Come in my son," said Grandma beaver when Jerry rapped on their house. Jerry came in and told them why his father had sent him.

Grandpa beaver talked to Jerry for a long time and Jerry was so amazed at the things he said, he could hardly believe it. Away he went back to his own house. "What's news?" asked his father when Jerry had recovered his wind after his fast swim. "Oh! let me tell you" panted Jerry. "I'll tell you just what Grandpa said." "Of course", replied his father. "That's just what I want you to do."

"What you smelled," said Jerry as he puffed out his chest with a show of as much importance as if he had made the discovery himself – "was coffee and bacon cooking on a fire." It's trappers, father – trappers come to catch us and sell our fur," and his voice was shaky. "Oh yes," said his father "now I remember. Once before there were trappers here but they are stupid creatures, not nearly as smart as we are. Do not be afraid." "But father," cried Jerry, "these are not ordinary trappers, they are the Howlenhammer Kids." "You mean the Whoopenhollar Kids" said his father. "Yes, I've heard of them and we must be careful. What else did your Grandpa say?" "He said he watched them all day yesterday as they made their camp and today he says they will start to build a cabin for the winter."

"Then," said his father, "they really mean business, but it will be quite a while before they put out their traps and in the mean time, my boy, you have a lot to learn about traps and how to keep out of them. Now come with me and we will watch them work." "But I was going to plaster the front room today like you told me to do last week," said Jerry, remembering all of a sudden what a safe place his home was. His father frowned at him. "If you have waited a week, it could wait another day and besides your mother did it yesterday."

So away went Jerry swimming behind his father as they made their way around the edge of the big pond keeping out of sight by staying close to the bank. When they came to the place where the water ran into the pond, they crawled out on the bank and made a circle to get on higher ground above the camp of the Whoopenhollar Kids. From this position, they could watch without being seen.

Already the Whoopenhollars were cutting trees to build their winter cabin and Jerry's father talked to him while they watched the kids work. Jerry became so interested that he forgot to be scared. It was the first time he had ever seen animals like these that walked around on their hind feet and that carried something in their front feet which they used to cut down trees instead of using their teeth. And what a queer way to build a house and what an awful job it must be not to have a pond to float their logs in.

"You see what stupid things they are," said Jerry's father. "They carry a lot of things around in their front feet, and never use their heads. They can't live in this cold water as we do and they can't live on land as our friends the deer do, with out building a fire to keep warm and to cook that awful smelling food. They need fur like we have and so they try to catch us and take our hides. They make more noise than our friends the squirrels, with all their jabbering and yet, they can't run up a tree and get their food from the pine cones as the squirrels do." "But still you have to be careful and keep away from these awful traps that they set. Only foolish beaver get into them and you need not be caught if you watch your step."

And so Jerry watched them putting log after log up on top of each other, pounding, chopping and sawing, until he became tired of watching such queer things. His father couldn't keep him still much longer so they crawled back to their pond and swam home.

Jerry was a sad little beaver. He had always romped and played from one end of the big pond to the other but soon he would have to give up playing because his father had said he must learn to go carefully or he would lose his coat. And so with out knowing it, Jerry was really growing up to be a wise beaver.

Dear Kids

Jerry Beaver sat watching the first snow fall he had ever seen. It came down so softly through the branches of the trees that were now shedding leaves of yellow and gold and red. He liked to see it cling to his fur and being used to cold water he never thought of the snow or cold at all. And when he moved around on the bank of the big beaver dam he left funny little tracks just like he did in the mud.

He had made several trips up the stream to watch the Whoopenhollar Kids build their winter cabin and he was becoming quite a brave little beaver. He had also watched them once when they came down to look at the big dam and he could hear them talk. What a queer language! He wished he could know what they were talking about. But he watched closely and saw one of the kids point to the beaver houses and again when he pointed to a tree that Jerry cut down the night before.

He swelled up with pride when one of the boys picked up a chip from the tree. It was a large chip and Jerry was becoming proud of his teeth and the way he could cut chips out of a tree.

As he sat there thinking, he wondered too when the boys would put out their traps. Maybe it would be O.K. to stroll up to the cabin and take another look, so off he started; but almost as quickly he stopped! Behind him were those funny little tracks. He thought a minute – no that wouldn't do. It is only when you feel safe that you leave tracks so he slid off the bank into the water, not with a splash as he would like to do but without any noise whatever and soon he was paddling up to the inlet of the big dam and a little later he crawled along the edge of the running stream; his fuzzy body almost out of sight in the water. From a low place in the bank he poked up his head and watched. Always there was something new to look at and although he couldn't even guess what some things were for, he liked to watch and learn.

He had seen the Whoopenhollar boys finish the cabin, then dig a big hole in the side of the hill beyond the cabin, afterward making another little cabin inside the hole and covering it all over with the dirt they had dug out leaving only a doorway in the front. Next, they all started to carry things and put them in this funny house under the dirt. "Ah, storing food for the winter just as we do," Jerry had thought. "That one is easy, even Tiny, the muskrat could figure that out."

But now as he looked he saw things that were not so easy to understand. How could little Jerry be expected to know about the skis that hung under the eaves of the cabin, the snow shoes on the wall or the sled that stood up on the ends of its runners, its top almost as high as the door? And right then that same door opened and Jerry ducked his head so quickly it almost went out of sight in the fur around his neck, but slowly he raised it again and watched the one Whoopenhollar kid that was different from the rest. She was sweeping out the cabin and now that Jerry could see inside – what a lot of things were there that he had yet to learn about. The rifles hanging on wooden pegs instead of the buck horns that would soon be nailed up on the logs, the double bunks in one corner of the large cabin and the cot in another corner covered with blankets of very bright colors.

Because Jerry could only watch (thru) through the door he could not see all the things that belong in a cabin but they were there just the same, for the Whoopenhollar Kids knew their business and they had packed in to the mountains, everything they would need for the long winter. There was the light cook stove in the corner near the door and across from it the table which the boys had made themselves from poles split in half and finished smooth with a draw knife. The shelves, too were made the same way and now they held tin dishes and many cans of things that the girl kept all nicely stacked up and in rows that would have looked to Jerry, if he could see it, like a lot of tree stumps close together. The girl finished sweeping the snow away from the doorway and stopped to look up at the falling snow. Then brushing the snow flakes from her pretty hair she went inside and closed the door. Jerry's sharp ears could hear her talking to one of her brothers who had been sitting by the table sewing a shoulder strap to a pack sack with a buckskin string.

The Whoopenholler Kids Winter Cabin

Jerry wondered where the other boys were. There must be some of them gone he reasoned or he surely would have seen them. Very soon again the door opened and two boys came out and went to a big wood pile where one of them started splitting more wood while the other carried it in the cabin and piled it behind the door. Jerry's animal instinct told him there were only the three people at the cabin and having learned all he expected to for one day, he started noiselessly down the stream towards his home in the big dam.

Today he had not seen the funny looking burros that had packed so many things to the cabin. Whenever the burros had loads on their backs some of the boys were always with them so Jerry reasoned that wherever the burros had gone to, so had the other two boys.

That night as he curled up in his cozy house, he thought about lots of things until he finally dropped off to sleep, never realizing that each day he was thinking harder and harder and the thinking was making him a wise little beaver who would soon be able to take care of himself.

As long as Jerry was sure there was no danger he could not keep away from his daily trips up the creek to watch the Whoopenhollars. Two days had gone by since the snow had started to fall and now it was so deep it came to the top of Jerry's back and he was almost 10 inches high when he humped his back to show his mother how big he was. On the third day the sun came out and Jerry, as usual, made his trip up the creek. It was late in the afternoon. Jerry had had to work at home in the morning peeling bark from the limbs of trees to store the bark for winter food. Now he hurried faster than ever because he heard noises like coyotes barking, only he knew coyotes real well and was sure that was not it.

He had just found one of his good hiding places in the stream near the cabin when he realized that whatever the noise had been it had something to do with the cabin because the girl and her two brothers were standing outside and looking up the trail that came through the tall trees. Again he heard that noise and a moment later, around a bend in the trail came a string of six big dogs, one behind the other, all with harness on them and pulling a long sled with bundles and boxes tied on to it.

The other two boys were trotting along behind the sled and the first one carried a light pole which he used to push on the sled when the dogs were pulling hard.

The sled came to a stop and some of the dogs sat on their haunches and whined while others stood up and wagged their tails. The girl patted each dog on the head and rubbed his ears and talked to them. The boys were talking too, all at once, because that is the way the Whoopenhollar kids always do. "Just like squirrels and magpies," thought Jerry as he listened to all the jabber.

As he listened, he watched, which was a beaver's way of doing things and he saw the boys unharness the dogs and unload the sled. The Whoopenhollars were so excited that they couldn't wait to carry the bundles in the cabin and Jerry had a chance to see a lot of new things. Pretty coats and caps and sweaters and then mittens and overshoes. Lots of parcels too that were wrapped in pretty paper. Two brand new rifles and two new pair of snow shoes and then the biggest box of all was opened and Jerry only had to look for a moment before he understood what he saw there! His father and mother had told him and even drew pictures in the mud of these things that the boys took out of the big box. It was a sad little Jerry that turned and made his way slowly toward his home. Jerry had seen more traps than his father had even told him there were in the whole world.

Kids – Can't seem to finish this. You'll have to wait.

Dear Kids

It was several days before Little Jerry the beaver made another trip up the creek to watch the Whoopenhollars. Jerry was not exactly frightened. He was just determined to keep his fur and as the winters where Jerry lived were cold he really needed that fur. So Jerry stayed pretty close at home and all the time his little brain was busy.

And so were the Whoopenhollar kids busy, for there was much to do if their winter was to be a success for them.

That evening after the two boys had arrived with the dog team the cabin was a regular work shop. So many things had to be unpacked and straightened up. There was dog harness to mend and clean; rifles to be cleaned and oiled and lots of cartridges to be put away on the home made shelves. The boys greased their boots and sharpened their hunting knives while the girl made some candy and mended the boys clothes. What a difference there was between that cabin and the other trappers cabins! So neat and clean. For the girl always went with her brothers and the boys would not think of going without her. Nor did she stay at the cabin all the time for on many trips she would be gone all day with them and the boys were always ready to help get supper when the party returned to their comfy cabin. They ate their candy and talked over the work for the next day.

"It is cold enough now for meat to keep quite awhile," said Billy as he reached for another piece of candy. "We ought to see tomorrow where the deer are and maybe pick up tracks of fur bearing animals and get some of these traps out."

"Oll, gob blub ging," Frank tried to say through a mouth full of candy and finally got the track clear, "somebody has to build a shelter for these dogs. John and I had a hard trip taking the jacks out of here and a harder one coming back with the sled. If John will help me we will stay in and build this tomorrow, my legs are sure tired." "O.K. with me," said John and rubbed a swollen hand. John and Frank had come on to a bee tree down in the low lands on their trip up with the dogs. They had smoked out the bees and gotten a pail of good wild honey but in the getting, John had become stung on the hand by a mad bee. Frank had started to kid John about letting a little bit of a bee hurt him, but as he backed away keeping his eye on the bees, Frank fell over the dogs and almost spilled the honey. "Anyway we got the honey," said John with a grin "and Frank had to untangle himself from the harness. "What's the matter Frank, didn't the dog harness fit you?" Glenn wanted to know.

The boys crawled into their bunks early and Jean took the lamp to her cot in the corner when she was ready for bed she turned out the light and said good night to her brothers.

Outside, a cold white moon was coming up over the mountain. It threw its silvery beams in the cabin window and spread a soft light over the colored Indian blankets on the girl's cot. A coyote yapped at the moon with his sharp barks and the dogs huddled against the side of the cabin, stirred and growled but settled back to sleep again.

Jean put steaming pancakes and bacon in front of the boys soon after day light and made up a couple of lunches for Billy and Glenn who were going hunting. After the second helping of these, the boys got up from their home made stools, put on their sheepskin coats and took their rifles down from the wall. Billy slipped a piece of buck skin string into his pocket and they started out, first telling the others which direction they intended to go. Boys who live a great deal in the forest always tell one another where they are going just in case someone may look for them and Billy was used to doing this even though there was snow on the ground and it would be easy to follow his tracks. Billy and Glenn followed the sled tracks up the valley a short way and then turned off to follow a game trail up a broad canyon.

Tracks were everywhere in the snow. Most of them were made by rabbits and squirrels but often they crossed the tracks of mink and marten near the creek and some beaver tracks near small dams. Bobcat and coyotes had been there too and their tracks showed where they had wound in and out of the brush in their hunt for rabbits and field mice.

Billy and Glenn took careful note of all these for here was a canyon where they should make a fair catch with their traps. Tracks of deer showed where a bunch had come down from the hillside to drink at the creek.

On the boys went, studying every sign of wild life that lived in the vast mountains so far away from the cities. Some grouse flew up in a spruce tree and Glenn, who carried a 22 rifle, got one of these, and a short way from there he bowled over a snowshoe rabbit. "Hang them on a tree limb and we will pick 'em up on the way back," said Billy.

The boys found a sunny spot against a large rock near the upper end of the canyon and there stopped to eat their lunch. Having finished that, they got up to go when a whistling snort made them turn to look and a small buck came bounding out of the timber. He raced down the hill leaping the fallen timber with ease. Billy's 30-30 cracked sharply but the deer ran on. Billy threw down on the rifle lever, flipped in another shell with lightening speed and fired again. There was a crashing of brush and tree limbs as the buck rolled over and over and then lay still.

The boys cleaned the buck, tied his hind legs to a pole with the heavy leather string Billy had and then bracing the pole against the ground, they lifted with all their strength and swung the deer into the branches of a large tree. There he hung against the tree, his legs tied up to a pole and his head not quite touching the ground.

"Well, there is plenty of meat for several days," remarked Billy. "It will take quite a lot, too for ourselves and the dogs; and now we had better be going, Glenn. Tomorrow when the meat is cold we will bring up some traps to set where we cleaned this buck and will take the meat to the cabin. His feet and his 3 point horns will make good gun racks or a place to hang our coats."

On the way back the boys followed a few tracks for a short way and made other detours but finally came to the place where hung the rabbit and grouse. They took these down from the tree and started on. Twice the boys were sure that they heard the dogs bark, but as this was common, they did not pay much attention to it.

As they came with in sight of the cabin they knew something had happened because there was no one in sight and not a sound came to them. The boys opened the door and went in – no one in the cabin. No dogs outside. Billy laid his rifle on the table and sat down on a stool. He began thinking of the places where his brothers and sister might have gone. He was sure there must be a good reason for them leaving if he could only think what it was.

Down at the dam in the big beaver pond, Jerry also was thinking. What had caused all the noise up at the cabin? Dogs barking and boys yelling louder than he had ever heard. He wanted to take a trip up there and watch but as he remembered all the traps he had seen only yesterday, he decided to stay away. Only one thing; Jerry knew he must be on the watch for and that was the day when the boys would come to set traps near his home. And on that day he would watch with both eyes wide open.

His sharp ears could still hear the barking of the dogs away beyond the ridge that ran down to a small point to form one end of the big dam. After awhile he could hear them no more and all was quiet in the forest, just like it had always been before the Whoopenhollars came.

And Jerry beaver wondered if he had seen the last of the boys and the little girl who had built their cabin home so near to his own.

Dear Kids,

This is an awful story. I can't seem to come to the end of it. But maybe you don't want to hear anymore, anyhow, anyway.

Daddy

Dear Kids

"I suppose the quickest way to find Frank, John and Jean is to look for them," said Billy to his brother Glenn, and picking up their rifles they left the cabin. When they had gone beyond the cabin grounds where tracks were few they started in a wide circle around the cabin. In this way Billy knew he would come upon the tracks he was looking for sooner or later and he was right, for about half way around the circle he and Glenn found the tracks of the three Whoopenhollar kids.

The tracks showed that the kids were running and Billy was puzzled to know what it was all about, but he swung in the direction they were going, followed by Glenn.

After a few minutes walking he saw in the snow the place where two of the dogs had joined the tracks of the kids and farther on the rest of the dogs had joined in also so that now all the tracks were jumbled together.

Then Billy noticed a spot of blood in the snow and a little farther on, another. What awful thing could have happened to his brother or sister? Could something have been chasing Jean and hurt her? – and the boys and dogs – were they running to catch up and save her?

Billy was indeed a worried boy, but turning around quickly he went back on the tracks to where the four dogs had joined the trail. Being careful not to step in the tracks himself he went slowly along watching closely the tracks made by the dogs. Then a big smile came across his face. "Come here Glenn and take a look," he yelled. "Now here is the whole story written in the snow – not very long after dinner, the dogs smelled a mountain lion and started chasing him. The kids at the cabin heard the dogs and they took a short cut through the timber and came on to the trail of the dogs. You can tell that, because the kids tracks are on top of the dog tracks. Either the lion is hurt or else it is one of the dogs. Lets hurry along and perhaps we can catch up and as we go, watch for a track with a spot of blood that hasn't been tramped out by the rest."

So away they went on a trot. Lots of places the tracks were scattered so that Billy could pick out each track separately and it was at one of these places that he stopped and examined a track which showed a blood stain in the snow beside it. "It is one of the dogs," said Billy. "I expect he rushed the lion too strong and the lion turned to fight rather than go up a tree. If the kids are lucky, the dogs will tree that big pussy cat in a mile or so. The dog can't be hurt much as it doesn't seem to hinder his running."

The country now was getting rougher and it was necessary for the boys to slow up. As they stopped to get their breath they heard the dogs bark away off in the distance. Such yelping! Billy knew how excited the dogs must be. "We hardly expected to go for a nice little run after hunting most of the day, but I guess our legs can take it, eh Glenn?" "Sure" said Glenn. "Let's go."

They stopped often now to listen and each time the barking of the dogs sounded closer. "The dogs have stopped running or else we wouldn't be able to hear them any plainer than at first," remarked Billy, "and that means just one thing – they have run that Kitty up a tree as sure as you're a foot high. What a nice pet he will make for you, Glenn" "No thanks__you can have him," was Glenn's reply. "Now isn't that just too bad, I'll bet he has the nicest long sharp teeth and such pretty claws with big hooks on them – sure you don't want him Glenn?"

The sharp crack of a rifle echoed across the valley. "That sounds like Frank's rifle and I think that is the last of your lion kitty. Now that you mentioned it, I believe he WOULD make a nice pet – from now on," and Glenn's grin stretched beyond all bounds of reason.

Frank and John were just finishing the skinning of the lion when the other boys came up. "What's the big idea, getting us all worried and hunting for you all afternoon?" said Billy, his eyes twinkling. "I notice that you didn't spend much time wondering which direction to hunt us," said John. "If you couldn't follow the tracks of one lion, six dogs and three people, then I think you better do all you're trapping for mice in Jean's pantry." Billy laughed and laughed. He was the oldest of the Whoopenhollar kids and one of the best trappers.

Jean was sitting on a log running her fingers through the thick hair on one of the dogs who lay panting beside her. Billy noticed the dark red streak on the upper part of his front leg, and went over to look at the wound. "Did the cat scratch you, Ham-bone?" he said to the dog who thumped his tail on the snow and licked Billy's hand when the boy touched his leg.

"I tried to bandage it with a handkerchief," said Jean "but he pulled it off with his teeth" and Billy said, "Ham-bone is O.K. He can heal the cut by licking it."

Ham-bone was the leader of the dog team and was the best and strongest of all the six large dogs. Ham-bone was also Jean's pet and when he was not in the harness with the other dogs, he liked to be with her, though he sometimes went lion hunting with the boys. Jean had her own small sled and when the trail was packed hard with snow, Ham-bone could pull her easily alone and Jean had lots of fun in the forests that other girls never even know about.

All the dogs were named because of some thing that fitted their nature or their likeness. "Ham-bone" was never happier than when he could lie at Jean's feet and gnaw a ham bone. "Trailer" had a good nose for following trails and for tracking. "Snow boy" was the best dog in deep snow and when helping to pull the big sled through a snow drift he always came through with his tail wagging. Then there was "Pudding". He was the youngest dog of all and this was his first winter in the harness. "Pudding" got his name when he was a puppy. Jean had tipped over a bowl of chocolate pudding and the pup got bowl, pudding and all upside down on his head. Another dog was named "Trouble" and this name fitted him as none other could. As a pup he was always in the way. He had scars on his feet where he had been caught in the boys traps and often the boys had had to pull porcupine quills out of his nose. One day he had chased a weasel into a hollow log. He was wearing a collar because the boys often tied him up to keep him out of trouble. The dog squeezed his head and part of his body into the log. The collar on his neck caught on a knot inside the log and the dog couldn't go ahead and he couldn't back-out so of course the boys had to split the log to get him out. He was getting to be an old dog now but still he was trouble. When the snow caked into ice between his hairy toes, he tried to chew it out and that is something that no harness dog should ever do. Chewing on his toes made them sore and often the boys had to make moccasins of buckskin to put on his feet. These were easily made – just a pouch with a drawstring to hold them on. But "Trouble" was a big strong dog and when his feet were kept in good shape he could pull all day and never seemed to get tired and so the boys would not think of parting with him.

One other dog – "Bunny" and of course he got that name because he was so fond of chasing rabbits. He seldom ever caught one but it made no difference. He chased them to see them run. His favorite pose was to sit on his haunches the way a rabbit always does. Although "Bunny" was a big dog he was smaller than the others. His place in the harness was next to the sled.

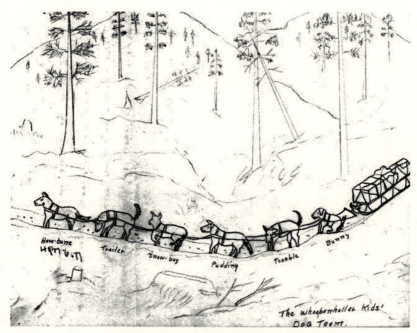

The Whoopenholler Kids Dog Team

The kids did not follow back on their own tracks very far. Where they had crossed the big creek before, they now took the trail that led up the stream. The stars were coming out like tiny campfires in the sky when the kids passed the big beaver dam on their way up to the cabin.

Jerry had heard them coming and was hiding among the sticks and logs in the dam. His keen eyes, used to darkness, took in every detail of the strange procession. The lion skin hanging over one boys shoulder, the rifles in their hands – Jerry knew now that rifles were made to kill with and those animals that looked like coyotes, that could pull a sled – they could also kill, for he had heard them chasing the lion. Just another lesson in Jerry's life but how well he learned his lessons.

"Trailer" stopped and sniffed the breeze, then came straight toward Jerry. Jerry slid silently under water out of sight and still under water he swam to his home and as he swam he smiled to himself.

I don't know what is the matter with this story kids – Looks like it just never will end.

Love from Daddy

Dear Kids

The next morning after the lion hunt, Billy helped Frank and John with the dog shelter that the two boys had nearly finished. It was just a lean-to, built against the cabin and had a canvas hanging over the entrance.

After this was done the boys hitched up five dogs to the sled and started after their venison. "Ham-Bone", the lead dog was left with Jean. His leg was a trifle stiff from the wound the lion had given him and so today "Trailer" was leading the team. Jean had a lunch ready for them and this, they had tied on to the sled, along with a dozen assorted traps.

They set a few Number One traps for mink along the creek and a couple of Number One and a halfs where they saw signs of marten; and finally came to the place where hung the three point buck. Here they ate their lunch and set out four Number Two double spring traps for red fox and any other animal that would come to nose around the place where they had cleaned the buck.

The last day and night had not been the least bit cold and the snow was melting. The sled runners sometimes cut to the ground, weighed down with their load of meat. To make matters worse there was no regular trail in this canyon and the boys found it hard to keep the sled right side up. The dogs panted and strained at their tugs as the sled runners hit the gravel but where the going was fair it was no load for these strong dogs.

Arriving at the cabin they skinned out the venison, cut it into quarters and covered it with clean burlap so the camp birds could not get to it and then hung three quarters in a tree high enough to be out of reach of the dogs. The fourth quarter they took in the cabin and cut it into steaks and roasts ready for cooking. Jean picked out some steak for their supper and Billy took the rest to their screen cooling box nailed on the outside of the cabin, first sorting out rib bones and scrap meat for the dogs.

In this northern country where the Whoopenhollars were trapping the game season lasted nearly all winter and beaver trapping was a good business but in some other places beaver are not plentiful and so of course they are protected from people who would trap them. Real trappers would not set out traps in such a country because they couldn't catch enough beaver to pay for their trouble, and besides no real trapper and hunter likes to see wild game getting less and less each year. So when this does happen, trappers put away their traps.

It was the next day after the kids had brought in the venison that Jerry Beaver was watching the cabin from his hiding place in the stream when he realized that the kids were getting ready to put out lots of traps.

Jerry had to be unusually careful now on his trips up the stream because of those awful dogs. By instinct he knew he must not be in the creek when the wind was blowing from him toward the cabin. Much as Jerry hated the smell of those dogs he knew it was safer for him if the breeze blew the dog smell toward him. Mostly the dogs stayed where the kids were but one time while he was watching on that very day, one of the boys had come to the creek for a pail of water. The dogs had come close to the bank, two of them, and although Jerry had slid into a dark hole under the bank and water was over the top of him his heart was in his mouth. There was the boy so close to him dipping water in the pail. After the boy and dogs had gone, Jerry thought of getting back home as fast as he could, but changed his mind when he remembered he had come up the creek to learn what he could and besides – wasn't Jerry growing to be a big beaver? And reasoned Jerry, a beaver that was a "fraidy cat" wouldn't learn anything by hiding in his home. So Jerry got up all the courage in his little body and crawled out of the dark hole that had hid him so well.

One of the boys was mixing some stuff in a small wooden barrel and later Jerry saw him put in the hide of the deer and also the lion. Jerry doubted if he could ever figure out what that was for but we know, of course, that the boy was soaking the hides in a tanning compound and days later he would dry them and rub them soft to make leather of the buck-skin and a rug out of the lion hide.

But Jerry was more interested in the other boys for they were sorting out traps in sizes they wanted to set that day. Gracious! such a lot of shiny new traps, and what a pity Jerry could not understand what the kids said.

"That big beaver dam looks like easy money to me," said Frank as he tried the double springs of a new Number Two beaver trap, "and on down the creek are dam after dam." And Frank tossed the Number Two on to a pile of other beaver traps with a clatter and jingle of chains. "We ought to make two or three catches in every good dam," agreed John "and a half dozen in the big dam." added Billy as he started stuffing unwanted traps back in the box.

Jerry watched them hang the traps over their shoulders by the chains. "Comin' Glenn?" asked Billy, and Glenn took another poke in the barrel with his stick, for good measure and watched the tanning fluid ooze over the hides like clothes in a wash tub. He seemed to be satisfied for he went to the cabin door, picked up his rifle and trotted after the others.

Jerry waited no longer! For the boys were headed straight for the big dam and he must beat them there. How he scampered along the creek – sometimes under water, sometimes only at the edge of the water, but always out of sight against the bank of the stream and soon he was at the inlet of the big dam and out of sight under the water.

But Jerry did not go to his house to hide out. Oh No! This was the time he had been watching for and he did not intend to miss it so swimming under water to the opposite side of the dam from the trail he came up under a clump of sticks and brush where the bank over hung the water.

He stuck his head through the tangle, hooked his front paws over a stick just under the water and waited.

Across the pond he saw the boys stop at the first mud slide they came to. "Oh Heck!" thought Jerry, "Father and I still have some small logs and sticks to bring down that slide. It is one of our best slides and now they are going to set traps there." And Jerry was right, for already Billy was cutting off a piece of wire about twelve feet long from a roll he had carried on his shoulder. This done, he took a pair of pliers from his pocket and twisted one end of the wire around a good sized rock. Then Frank handed him a piece of soft iron shaped like a barb which Billy clamped on to the wire, squeezing it tight with the pliers, about two feet from the rock. As John held up the chain on a beaver trap, Billy stuck the other end of the wire through the ring on the end of the chain and tied the wire to a small stump on the very edge of the water. Holding on to the trap Frank picked up the rock and tossed it into the pond – Splash! It made more noise than Jerry could make when he dived off of the highest bank around the big dam. Waves of water rippled across the pond from the splash and reaching Jerry, these waves rolled up gently against his chin.

As the rock settled down on the mud in the deep water and the wire stretched tight, two of the boys squeezed the trap springs down, spread the jaws and set the trigger. Then with sticks they pushed the trap on the mud until it was well down under the water, the chain ring sliding along on the wire. And the first beaver trap was set! Jerry watched, his eyes getting bigger and bigger. There was more to this trapping business than he had ever dreamed.

On the boys went setting a trap at each likely looking place, and Jerry, watching, forgot everything else, which is something a wise beaver shouldn't do. Jerry felt a sick feeling in his stomach as something grabbed his flat tail and pulled him through the brush and out of sight under the water!

Dear Kids – what awful thing happened to Jerry? Is this a good place to end the story? You'll have to let me know.

Dear Kids

Jerry Beaver was in a bad fix. He tried to turn and fight this new enemy but he was hopelessly tangled in the brush and roots that lay under the water. At last he found himself dragged beneath the brush so that he could twist his body around and with his sharp teeth showing, he made ready to fight for his life – and what a surprise he got! It was his own father!

"How you scared me!" said Jerry, panting when he came to the surface of the water where he COULD pant. "I was watching the Whoopenhollar Kids set traps." "Yes, I know," replied his father. "I was watching them and you too."

Jerry didn't have any more to say about it, but he resolved right there never to be caught napping again.

"What shall we do?" asked Jerry anxious to change the subject. "They have put traps in all the places we always use." "And where did you think they would put them?" asked his father and Jerry felt silly for saying such a thing.

Jerry and his father found a comfortable place against the over hanging bank where there was no brush and they could dive under the water at a moments notice. Then his father began talking.

"We must begin now to find new places to cut timber and make new mud slides to bring our sticks to the water and when traps are set, there we will make more new ones. Within a few weeks it will grow cold and ice will come on the pond. By that time we will have all the green sticks we need for winter food and we will be much safer."

"And maybe the trappers won't catch any beaver after all," said Jerry. "I'm sorry to say, they will, "replied his father. "There are always some beaver as well as other woodland people who are always getting into trouble. These beaver learn to build a house and a small dam and how to store food but that is about as far as some of them go. They never really pay much attention to what is going on around them." "Couldn't we go down the creek to the other dams and warn all the beaver about these trappers?" asked Jerry

"We have been passing the word down the creek every day, my boy," was his father's answer. "But some of our people listen for awhile and then forget; others just don't seem to care for they go on in the same old way until it is too late. Of course there are plenty who do watch their step and it is from these wise ones that we up here in the big dam depend on news from the rest of the creek. But just today when cousin Ned sent word that the trappers were coming, one beaver said that if your cousin would patch that hole in the corner of the dam by his place, instead of trying to give so much advice, then the other beavers down the creek would feel safer. Of course we know there is no danger of the big dam breaking and washing out the smaller dams below us, and Ned was repairing it anyway until he got a touch of rheumatism and had to take sun baths on top of his house. But that is the way of some people and even though they won't take our advice let us show them that we can take theirs if it is GOOD advice and we will swim down to Ned's place and finish his work for him."

"But suppose the trappers have set traps at the hole where Ned was working," protested Jerry. "Please remind me to punch Ned in the nose if I put my foot in a trap at his place," replied his father and Jerry had to laugh though he had to admit to himself that it was his own foot he was worrying about.

After the work was finished at Beaver Ned's place, Jerry and his father swam to their home. Jerry was hungry after working all day and watching for the Whoopenhollar kids at the same time, and when his mother called him to supper he didn't have to be coaxed. She passed him a nice fat stick covered with juicy green bark and Jerry started peeling it and eating the bark without raising any fuss about all the knots.

"Now let us go across the pond and take a good look at these traps," said Jerry's father when supper was over. Jerry had gotten over the scare his father had given him so once again he was the brave little beaver and getting wiser all the time. Without a word of protest he dived down in the water to the door of his home and came up on the outside to look and listen before he left such a safe place.

When his father had come up beside him they started swimming away and it pleased Jerry to notice that his father had not stopped to look for danger but had trusted Jerry's keen eyes and ears to be alert.

Then they came near to where the boys had set one of their traps. Jerry's heart beat a little faster when he thought how near he was to danger. His father said, "Now this wire which you see there is fastened one end to a stump and one end to a rock and it is put there to drown you when you get in this trap." – "You mean ME," said Jerry and his jaw fell so low it came close to getting unjointed.

"Well I hope not you," answered his father. "I mean just any beaver that happens to get into it, and though we beaver can stay under water a long time we must come to the top for air sometimes. Now you wait here while I get a stick and I will show you how it works."

So Jerry's father scampered up the bank and soon came back dragging a stick held between his sharp teeth. And Jerry watched closely when his father pushed the stick toward the trap which was only partly buried in the mud. What would the trap do? Jerry almost expected the trap to jump out of the mud and grab him! The end of the stick pushed against the trigger of the trap and SNAP!! The stick jumped in the water as the trap jaws came together – Jerry also jumped! Gracious! The trap had grabbed the stick as though it were mad. "Now," said Jerry's father, if your foot was in that trap the first thing you would try to do would be to dive into deeper water and out of sight. Just watch this" – and Jerry's father took the end of the stick in his teeth and started down into deeper water dragging the trap which was of course still hanging on to the other end of the stick. And now Jerry saw the ring in the end of the trap chain sliding along the wire. When the ring came to the barbed clamp, it slid over it, but there it was, and it could not come back for the barb held it from going back up the wire.

"But why do they fix them to drown a beaver?" said Jerry. "Because," replied his father, "we beaver are strong enough to twist a foot out of a trap if we have time enough, but in this way we would drown before we could do it." Jerry thought about this for a few minutes. If he had been a human being like the Whoopenhollar boys he would have hated them for trying to catch him, but Jerry knew only the ways of woodland people, and he supposed it was the way of the Whoopenhollars. They must catch beaver and other animals in order to live, just as the coyote must catch the rabbit or chipmunk and though it couldn't be said that Jerry liked the boys, still he liked to watch them and learn how to keep out of their way.

Jerry's father guessed what Jerry was thinking about and he said with a smile, "that is the way of the world, my boy. No matter who you are, you must learn to take care of yourself and the better you learn to do it, the longer you will live and be happier, too."

After the Whoopenhollar boys had set their beaver traps they came back to their cabin. The sky was clouding over and some flakes of snow began to fall. "We must get in some more wood right away," said Billy. And John said, "I want to go up the creek and set a few mink traps. I'll help you when I get back." So picking up his rifle and traps, John set off.

About a mile from the cabin John had set his last trap. There he crossed the creek and decided to go back that way while looking for signs of other animals. He was surprised to find tracks of two cub bear and so fresh that the tracks were on top of the new snow. "Maybe I'll get me a bear," said John to himself and began following the tracks. Around a bend in the creek he saw them – two fat cubs. They jumped into the brush before John could get a shot so he ran after them.

Suddenly, there was a roar behind him and John turned to see a big angry bear charging straight at him.

Dear Kids – It looks like John is in a bad fix now. I wish you would write to me and tell me how to get him out. Daddy

Dear Kids

John was in about the tightest spot he had ever been and that was saying a great deal, for John had hunted and trapped and lived with his brothers and sister in pretty wild country and though he was just a boy he knew how to take care of himself in most places. Still, when John turned to face an angry bear he knew this was one time when only quick action would save him, and plenty quick it had to be.

Throwing his rifle to his shoulder he drew a hurried aim at the big shaggy animal. This was no time for trembling hands. The sharp crack of his Winchester echoed down the narrow valley as he pressed the trigger and the other boys down at the cabin stopped sawing wood to listen.

John saw the bear go down but only for a second and then madder than ever she came up again and staggering from side to side she came at him. That second was long enough for John to work the lever on his rifle and as he flipped in a new cartridge, he realized his first shot was not quite true and he now faced a wounded bear which was worse than ever. If his next shot failed would he have time for a third one? John doubted it. Unless he could slow the bear up again with this shot he knew he had spent his last winter with a dog team and a trap line. John could see the white bead of his rifle sight through the "V" near his eye. The bead was now right in line with his eye and the bears head and John's finger once more came back on the trigger.

Down at the cabin, Billy and Frank pulled the saw out of the cut made in the big dry log and Billy remarked "John must have got a deer with those two shots in rapid succession, guess we better go up the creek and help him dress the meat." Frank hung the long saw up on the side of the cabin, and went in to get his hunting knife and a small piece of rope. On the way up the creek the boys talked of the snow storm, trapping and hunting and other things that they were interested in.

John heard them on the trail across the creek and called to them. Imagine Billy and Frank's surprise to see John skinning a big bear. "Couldn't you find a bigger bear than that, John?" asked Frank with a grin. "I didn't find her," said John "She found me." and John began to tell them what had happened and how his second shot had stopped the mad bear just in time, and as the boys began to help with the skinning they knew that as long as the bear skin made a rug in their cabin, John would remember the thrill of that hunt

Three days more had gone by and it had snowed most of the time. The boys did not pay much attention to any of the traps except the beaver traps. Most animals do not move around much in a snow storm and the boys knew that lots of their traps would have to be pulled up out of the deep snow and re-set.

They spent most of their time cutting wood and making things that Jean wanted for the cabin. Crooked limbs of trees when peeled smooth made a chair with a back to it and a piece of deer skin made a softer seat on it. The wooden pack boxes were put one on top of the other and fastened together and made a cupboard and in the long evenings in the cabin, Jean sewed or read a book and the boys rubbed down the hides they intended to keep By rubbing them with a stone they made them soft after they had tanned them and the lion skin was now spread out on the floor for a rug and the bear skin would soon be beside it.

As they worked in the evening on these things they talked and joked. Said Frank one evening, while stretching a beaver skin over a wooden frame to dry it, "It's sure funny about that big beaver dam. We have never caught a single thing there and that is the place we expected to get six or eight."

"Not only that," answered Billy, "but half of the traps there are sprung every day. I've heard of a coyote that would push dirt from off a bank and set off a trap and maybe these sprung traps in the big dam aren't just accidents."

"Well, I think that if a beaver is smart enough to spring the traps, he deserves to keep his fur" was Jean's way of putting it. "Just the same," spoke up Glenn "I'm going to try to find out why there is never a catch in those traps, and say," he added, "when are we going. to the trading post again?"

"I was thinking about that," answered Billy. "We should go in once more this winter before the snow gets too deep for the dogs and this storm ought to make it about right after it freezes down a little. I would like to put it off for a week or so more until we have a few more furs to take in and then we can bring back a sled load of the things we need to make our supplies just right for the rest of the winter."

When the snow storm cleared away it left a land covered with a deep white blanket. The boys were now out early and late setting new traps and re setting old ones. Where they had shot the buck deer they caught three red foxes and along the creek the mink and marten traps were doing good.

Their supply of fresh meat was getting low by now and as so many deer had moved down to lower country because of the big storm it was up to the boys to go after them. Frank came in one day about noon after covering a short stretch of trap line. "I came on fresh tracks of two elk," he told Jean as he pulled off his snow shoes and tapped them together to knock the snow out of the webbing. "I'm going after them. Pack food enough for three meals in my pack sack while I eat some dinner." "You shouldn't go alone, Frank, wait till the other boys come in or let me go with you," said Jean as she set a bowl of hot soup on the table to start Frank's dinner.

"Not this time, honey," he said. "The other boys will be tired when they come in and you ought to be here and I can't wait until tomorrow; but I wish you would tell them to track me up with the dog team tomorrow, early."

"Ham-Bone is the only dog here now. Do you want to take him with you?" Jean asked. "No, I haven't time to chew his food for him," answered Frank and looked down into his bowl of soup so Jean wouldn't see him grin. "You talk as tho' Ham-Bone was so old he was tooth less but he is still the best dog in the team and he knows more than all the rest put together." Ham-Bone, hearing Jean's voice came out of his shed and pawed at the door to be let in.

Frank finished his dinner, shouldered his light pack which contained a frying pan, small coffee can and cup and some food and extra matches. Next he rolled up a single wool blanket into a long roll that came over his shoulder and fastened together army style under his arm. Then he slid a belt ax and holster on to his cartridge belt and went out side to buckle on his snow shoes. "Good-By sister," he said as she handed him his gloves and rifle. "No, Ham-Bone, you stay here," he added as the dog started to follow. "Jean needs you more than I." Ham-Bone's tail stopped wagging and his ears drooped. It was the second time that day that Frank had told him to stay at the cabin and this time he felt as though he should go, as much as he liked to be with Jean.

About the middle of the afternoon Frank came upon the tracks he had seen in the morning and with a swish, swish of his webs he followed them over the rolling timbered country. Just before daylight was fading he came out on a ridge. Looking across the wide valley with its open parks spread out before him, he saw the elk walking slowly through the deep snow. They were nearly a half mile away and much too far for a shot.

As Frank watched them he thought "They are tired from traveling all day just as I am. I'll bet they bed down for the night in that thick timber just beyond them, and I'll be wise to camp here and come on to them lying down just at daylight. Before I could reach them now it would be dark." Frank stood as motionless as the big tree against which he leaned as he watched the elk go in to the groove of timber.

Still watching, he waited to see if they would come out on the other side. He didn't think they did but it was now getting so dusk he couldn't be quite sure, so he turned his weary steps along the ridge until he came to a wide over hanging rock with small bushy trees on either side.

"Not quite as cozy as the cabin but it'll do for tonight," thought Frank and he leaned his rifle against the rock and took off his snowshoes. With one of these he scooped the snow away from under the rock and then stood them up beside his gun. Pulling his belt ax from its holster he scouted around near his clearing for some dead wood. Finding this close at hand, he chopped up some small pieces using the dry centers to start his fire.

Soon it was blazing brightly and he put on larger pieces. He had taken his light pack off his back and now he began cutting boughs from nearby fir trees being careful not to take any from the trees nearest his clearing as these would serve as a wind break. His fire made a cheery light as he worked dragging in the boughs, and the flames licked up against the over hanging rock.

When the fire had died down to glowing coals he filled his coffee can with snow and set it on the fire. It was soon melted to water and he added more snow until he had a can half full of steaming water. Then he took his fry pan from the pack, set it on the fire and dropped a part of the venison steak he carried into it. He COULD get along on the meat and hot coffee but he spread out the rest of his pack on the boughs to see what he had – half a loaf of bread, a small can of beans (and before looking at the rest, he rolled the can into the fire with a stick), salt, a piece of bacon, his cup full of dried prunes wrapped over with a cloth, and his fork and spoon and the coffee was about all.

Frank smiled as he looked at it. "Jean knows her business," he thought. "There is plenty but not a pound too much to carry." Then he spied a small wax paper wrapped up. He opened it and there he found three cookies. Girls will be girls and they don't intend that a hunter's camp fire will make you forget them.

Frank dumped about a third of his coffee into the boiling water and set the can to the side of the fire where it would simmer and not boil over. When his steak was broiled he sliced off some bread with the long keen blade of his pocket knife and used the short heavy blade to open the bean can. Then he poured his coffee and squatting on the pile of boughs he tossed a few sticks of wood on to the fire to give him light and began to eat. How good food is when you are trail tired and hungry! Frank liked milk and sugar in his coffee. He also liked pie and whipped cream on pudding, but he never thought of it now.

After he had eaten, he put more snow in the coffee can and when it was warm he rinsed out his cup and fry pan and dried them with the cloth. This done he raked his fire out from under the over hanging rock. The ground underneath was now warm and he remade the fire a few feet away. Next he cut the smaller limbs and twigs from the green boughs and spread them like a blanket where the fire had been. Some more wood in larger pieces that would hold the fire, he soon rustled and his camp was made for the night.

Before rolling up in his blanket, he placed his rifle in the boughs beside him where it would keep dry and stood his webs on end in the snow some distance from the larger fire where the heat would not dry out and crack the raw hide lacing.

Five or six times in the night he rolled out to pile more wood on his fire as it died down and he became too cold to sleep. The stars twinkled over head and the stillness of the forest night was broken occasionally by the bark of a fox and once Frank heard the deep wailing howl of a wolf.

About the fourth time he rolled out to put wood on the fire, he got out his coffee can and cram(m)ed it with snow so that long before it was day light Frank had hot water and was out fixing his breakfast. Finishing that, it was short work to pack his things and start out on the elk trail again.

The snow reflected light enough for him to see the plain trail and he lost no time getting down into the valley. A faint light in the east told him that dawn was coming as he made his way slowly and carefully up the side of the hill where stood the grove of timber that he hoped concealed the elk.

Still some distance from the grove, he quit the tracks and made a wide circle in order to come in above it. Being a good hunter, Frank knew that deer and elk will bed down facing their tracks and they would be on the watch for any person or animal that might be tracking them to their bed. Frank also took note of the direction of the breeze before he decided to take the left side of the timber on his half circle trip around it.

When he was on the hill above the timber he looked again for tracks and with a satisfied smile as (he) saw the smooth snow, untracked, he settled down to wait a few minutes for a little more daylight, for he knew now that the elk were below him in the grove.

He squinted his eye along the sights of his rifle to test the light – not quite plain enough yet – just a few minutes more but he couldn't wait, so placing each snow shoe down carefully step by step he stole down through the timber without a sound. The elk had winded him and up went one pair of large antlers. In the dim light, Frank drew his sights down to the dark bulk below those tree-like horns and fired.

There was a crashing of brush and limbs as Frank saw the elk's horns sink down for an instant and then he seemed to come up with a bound and dash down through the trees. Franks disappointment was indeed great for he had tracked them far only to fumble his shot. He fired again at the running elk but the thick timber and the poor light made a bad shot of it. He started to run out of the grove where he could see the elk in open country and in his haste he caught his snow shoe in a dry limb that stuck just up above the snow.

He sprawled head first in the snow with such force that his rifle flew from his hand and went out of sight in the deep snow ahead of him. The web that had caught on the limb had broken the strap around his boot and was entirely off.

Frank got to his feet with his back against a tree. His pack and blanket were a snow ball mass so he threw the shoulder straps off and let the pack drop in the snow. The snow shoe still on one foot was twisted and he stooped to straighten it – and then – a long chill went up his spine for not sixty yards away a bull elk with lowered antlers was coming straight for him – so that was it – he had wounded one elk slightly and it was the other one that he had seen dashing away.

Poor Frank – his rifle gone, one snow shoe off, miles from his cabin and he faced a wounded bull elk.

Dear Kids, This is almost going too far. I'll be getting the Whoopenhollar Kids into so much trouble it will take all winter to get them out. I sure need some help – Dad

Dear Kids –

About the time that Frank was preparing his breakfast in the shelter of the over hanging rock, just before meeting up with the elk, John was harnessing the dogs for the trip to catch up with Frank. Billy and John were both going and Billy was packing a few things to eat and two blankets on the sled; as they were not sure that they could get back in one day even with an early start.

"What do you suppose is the matter with Ham-Bone?" said John. "I never saw him so anxious to get started on a trail." "I hope you will find Frank alright," Jean remarked, "but I couldn't help but worry about him and I think Ham-Bone feels the same way." "Oh rats," Billy said, "Frank is OK I only hope he got his elk."

John spoke sharply to the dogs and they jerked into line quickly – all except Bunny, who was dreaming of rabbits as usual and was almost yanked off of his feet. Jean hopped on the sled to ride a short distance and when she got off she waved to the boys and walked back to the cabin.

"Well, sleepy head," she said to Glenn who was just getting up, "What are you going to do today?" "I'm going to try to find out why we can't catch beaver out of the big dam and as long as the dam is probably in the same place as it was yesterday, I don't see any reason to get up two hours before daylight." Glenn dodged a pillow that Jean threw at him and strolled over to the wash bench.

As Billy and John passed the big beaver dam, Jerry was out to watch for them for he had heard the dogs early and knew something was up. But the boys only glanced at the ice where some of their traps were and sped on their way.

And what about Frank! – His hands were already on the strap that held the one snow shoe to his foot as he saw the bull elk coming in jumps thru (through) the snow at him. Quick as a flash he jerked the strap loose and like a monkey began climbing the tree beside him. The large sharp antlers of the elk crashed into the tree just as Frank pulled his feet up and out of the way. He then climbed a few feet higher to a good sturdy limb where he made himself a seat with one arm around the trunk of the tree.

"Whew!!" said Frank half aloud "That was a close shave", and he wiped his face with the sleeve of his free arm. "And now that I'm up a tree, I wonder how long it will be before the other boys get here. What if they too had some trouble and can't come for a day or so. What a fine mess – Doggone! I wish I had carried my six shooter on my belt even if they are extra weight," and so on Frank mumbled to himself.

The elk backed away from the tree, his eyes red and his nostrils flaring. Then spying Frank's pack that was dropped near the tree, he charged it. It caught on his horns and he tossed it off, then tramped it and charged it again until it was in shreds and he still jumped on to the pieces. In the scuffle, his sharp foot went thru (through) the snow shoe that Frank had pulled loose in the nick of time. It flopped around his leg as he stormed around the tree.

"Go find the other web and wear it too if it will do you any good," said Frank to the mad elk, but the elk had pulled his foot out and backed away, panting and with head lowered. He seemed to be content now just to stand there and keep Frank up the tree.

The sun came up and began it's trip across the sky and still the elk kept Frank treed, but from his high perch, Frank saw the long black dot on the snow that was the dog team and the boys as they came down the opposite side of the valley and then out of sight from him as they reached the bottom.

Frank wasn't sure just what the elk would do when he heard others coming – he didn't want the elk to get away and he didn't want his brothers to get into a jam in case the elk took a notion to stay and fight so a happy thought came to him. He wiggled out of his coat and came down the tree a short way. Then he yelled as loud as he could and waved his coat at the elk, who came at it with fury. In this way, Frank kept the elk busy and John and Billy, hearing Frank yell, came up and finished the elk.

Frank slid down the tree, looking rather sheepishly. "Well, well," said Billy. "I believe it is our brother Frank and he has been showing an elk how to climb trees." "Yes," answered John, grinning. "We have such nice trees around the cabin, I wonder why he must come so far just to climb trees." "You fellows go chase yourselves, will you?" said Frank and began digging around in the snow to find his rifle. As Frank began telling them how it all happened, they fell to work fixing up the meat to haul back on the sled.

Meanwhile, Glenn and Jean were spending some time at the big beaver dam. Glenn set a couple of mink traps on the bank near where the water poured thru (through) the sticks of the dam too fast to freeze. The beaver traps that were now under the ice, he re-set near open water. Most of them had been sprung as usual by Jerry himself and Glenn scratched his head in thought. "I guess it is too much for me to figure out," he said to Jean "There is a beaver in this pond that is too smart for the Whoopenhollars." They went back to the cabin and Glenn worked on the wood pile that always seemed to need attention.

It was after dark when the other boys came in, but after taking care of the dogs and the meat they sat around the stove and Frank told them again about his elk hunt so that Jean and Glenn could hear it. "I've got a job re-stringing the snow shoe that the elk tried to wear and I'm going to lace it with elk hide," said Frank and a howl of laughter went up from the others.

"And now it's about time to think of going to the trading post," Billy said. "Suppose we cover the best part of our trap line tomorrow and start in on the next day." "OK," replied Frank "John and I were there last, the time we brought out the dogs and left the burros, and so we will look after the traps and batch while you three make the trip How about it, John?" "OK with me as long as you don't expect me to sit up in trees to amuse an elk that" – but John got no farther for Frank leaped on to him and they rolled over on the cabin floor much to everyone's delight for it was all in fun.

The next day the boys took from one of their traps, as fine a silver fox as they had ever seen. "That fur alone will pay us for three weeks work," remarked Billy a he stroked the thick black and silver tipped fur, and with the rest of the furs we have, we're not doing bad at all."

All that day Jean was excited at the thought of going to the trading post. It was nearing Christmas time and she thought about all the pretty things she would see and buy. She would get Christmas presents for them all. She would see other girls at the post and there would be dancing and music and new people and new magazines and new talk and besides, just going somewhere was always fun. And so as the sled was being packed, the next morning she danced up and down with delight. She had put on all the things they would need for the trip which would take two days each way. The boys tied up their bundle of furs and roped it on the sled and hitched up the dogs. Ham-Bone would not be caught easily and when the boys finally did get hold of him he begged as hard as a dog knows how not to be put into the harness. "What's coming over that fool dog?" Frank said. "It sure beats me how he seems to know just what he wants to do." "Let him go," said Jean. "Our load is light and you don't need him. He can hike along with me and work on the heavier trip coming back."

"Oh, alright, but I think he is getting lazy," Billy remarked as he put Ham-Bone's harness on the sled.

Frank and John went up the trail with the others as far as the place where John killed the bear and then with several "Good bye's," they watched them until they disappeared around a bend in the trail.

Ham-Bone romped with Jean in the snow, going round and round her or showed his importance by poking his nose into a hole in a stump and blowing hard as though he expected to chase out a moose, or a grizzly bear.

The travelers had a long low range of mountains to cross. It was this range that lay back and beyond their cabin in the opposite direction from the big beaver dam. The kids had crossed this range about mid afternoon and started down the long easy grade on the other side. They pulled their skis off of the long sled and with no effort at all they coasted along with the sled as the dogs trotted, hardly pulling at all.

By evening they were down in the wide valley and crossing the rolling hills. Some small lakes frozen over were passed and they came to a wide stream. Picking a place where the wind had blown the snow from the ice, the kids started to make the crossing. Ham-Bone began barking wildly and chased down the side of the stream where some distance lower down he crossed. The other dogs chased after him before the boys could stop them and soon the sled and boys were also across. Ham-Bone again barked like mad as he raced back up the creek and Jean laughed and waved her hand at him. – too late Jean understood the dog's meaning, for out in the middle of the ice it broke with a crash-water spurted up through the big hole as Jean went out of sight in the icy depths.

Dear Kids, This is getting worse and worse; something's gotta be done. Daddy

Dear Kids –

The icy water had hardly gone over Jean's head when the brave dog Ham-Bone reached the hole and without stopping he leaped in after her. Billy and Glenn were now running as fast as they could up the ice and in their hearts was a big fear for their only sister, whom they loved and no wonder that they did, for without Jean the trails would be twice as lonely and the cabin only a cold shack to come to after long hours on the trap line As the boys saw the dog disappear in the water they wondered if the running stream would take both the dog and Jean under the ice and down the river, never to be seen again.

But before the water had time to pull Jean under the ice, Ham-Bone had clamped his teeth in the back of her coat and struggling hard he lifted her head above the water; and Jean, gasping for breath, grabbed the edge of the broken ice. When she tried to pull herself up, the ice broke off and she clutched at the new edge. Some boys would have rushed up to the hole and probably broken the ice again and fallen in also, but not the Whoopenhollar boys. Billy yelled to Glenn to get the tie rope off of the sled and then as he came near the hole he lay down on his stomach and wiggled along with outstretched arms. His weight was now spread over so much of the ice that it held him up and soon he was able to grasp Jean's hands. "Good boy, Ham-Bone. Hang on a little longer," encouraged Billy.

The other dogs hitched to the sled had followed Billy and Glenn and when Glenn turned to get the rope he found the sled was not far behind him. One end of the rope was tossed out to Billy who tied it around Jean under her arms and then he slid back to thicker ice and he and Glenn began pulling on the rope. The ice broke off several times in front of Jean as she tried to climb up but finally it held and up she came. Billy slipped the rope off of her and slid out again to tie it around the brave dog. Ham-Bone was eagerly waiting for it and before Billy could reach around him, he grabbed the rope in his strong teeth. "OK Boy! You know what you want as usual so just hang on with your teeth and we'll do the rest."

It was quick work to get Ham-Bone out and now the boys drove the dogs up the bank and over to the first thick clump of trees where they fell to work with all speed to build a fire. As the fire grew larger more wood was piled on and Jean stood dripping wet and shivering and still pale from her scare. The sled was unloaded, snow scooped away for a wide space around the fire and the boys helped Jean off with her wet clothes and wrapped her in blankets and she sat on the sled near the fire while the boys put up sticks and brush to hang her clothes to dry.

It was now evening and other things were made ready to camp for the night just as they had done many times before. Ham-Bone lay at Jean's feet, his thick hair steaming as it dried out. Jean patted him on the head then suddenly reached down and threw her arms around his neck and there were tears in her eyes as she said "Ham-Bone, dear old fellow, you are through being a common harness dog. You can turn that job over to Trailer and just take care of me, will you do that?" and Ham-Bone thumped his tail on the ground with all the energy he could. Billy spoke up as he stirred some soup over the fire. "He is yours, sister," and then added thoughtfully, "I guess he always was," and Glenn said, "Until he learns how to set traps and skin beaver, I guess I can get along without him." This made Billy and Jean laugh and soon all three were joking as though nothing unusual had happened; though Billy and Glenn often glanced at Ham-Bone and wondered how a dog could have so much sense; and as they lay in their blankets that night and looked up at the stars they said little prayers of thankfulness to a Heavenly Father who watches over a wilderness of forests and gives to His trapper children, great blessings, though such blessings may be hidden under the coarse ugly hair of a big dog.

It was late the next afternoon when the Whoopenhollar kids pulled into the Trading Post. Now, a trading post is something like a very small town and a place where trappers come to sell their furs or to trade them for the things they need – rifles, blankets, cartridges, coffee, sugar, in fact most anything that the kids could want. The trading post or store was a big log building where the trader lived and kept his goods. Scattered around in the clearing were several cabins and nearby flowed a large river partly frozen over. Small boats came up the river in summer with stores of things for the trading post from the large river towns.

The big trader and his wife came to the door with friendly smiles. "Well, well, here are our friends the Whoopenhollar Kids. Our boys and girls will be glad to see you. Just find you an empty cabin and unhitch, but you must have supper with us tonight," he said as they shook hands all around. "Thank you," said the kids. "We will be glad to." Now other people were coming out of their cabins when they heard all the neighborhood dogs barking at the kid's dog team. Some of the people the kids knew and some were strangers.

One man in particular, a stranger to the kids, Billy noticed. He was an old man with coarse dirty whiskers and ragged clothes and later on as Billy was caring for the dogs, he had a chance to see him close. The old man had a half crazed look in his eye and seemed to be sickly. Billy knew enough to be careful about taking up with strangers and this one especially, he didn't want anything to do with. The old man came over to where Billy was working.

"A right nice dog team ye got thar, son," he said. Billy couldn't tell by looking in the man's crazy eyes whether he just meant to be friendly or if he was scheming, but Billy answered politely, "Yes sir, they are pretty good dogs." "Whar be ye located?" the old man continued. Billy saw no reason not to answer the crazy old fellow. "On upper Beaver Creek, two days out." Billy plainly showed that he didn't care to talk to him but this did not discourage the old man who kept asking questions and watching the dogs and the long shiny sled. "I got me a shack down thar on the river," he poked his hand out of a ragged sleeve and pointed. "I'd like to have ye come down and see me." "Perhaps," answered Billy and picking up blankets and things, went into the cabin the trader's wife had told Jean to use, leaving the old man staring at the dogs.

"I don't like his looks," Jean whispered to Billy. "Nor do I," Billy answered. "I have an idea he would like to steal our outfit. Presently the old man wandered away and the kids began to think of other things. One of the trader's girls came in and Jean was glad to see her. They talked about everything under the sun. The girl had been down the river and couldn't wait to tell Jean about all the things she had seen in the cities.

The four of them went over to the traders as it was now supper time, and after they had enjoyed a fine meal, Billy and Glenn brought in their furs for exchange. Jean was already looking at everything in the store as the trader sorted out the different skins and wrote his price for each one and added up the list of figures. "$833.00," he said to Billy. "Not enough," said Billy. "I'll make it $850.00 even up," answered the trader. "Still not enough, I figured on getting $900.00 for those skins," Billy insisted. "Now listen, Billy," said the trader, "$850.00 is the best I can do. I've got to hold these furs until I get enough to pay for a trip down river and by that time the price may drop and I'll lose money." "Yes and the price may go up and you will double your money," Billy grinned at him, "but I'll tell you what, throw in one of those pups in the bargain and we'll close the deal." The trader scratched his head as he looked at five roly-poly puppies, playing on the floor.

"Well now, those are valuable pups, Billy and besides they belong to my kids." The girl with Jean heard her father and she called to her younger sister and two brothers. "Let's give the Whoopenhollar Kids one of the pups for Christmas," she said and the others agreed, and so their father reached for his ledger and entered a credit of $850.00 for the Whoopenhollars.

"Have you picked out what you want, sister?" asked the boys after they had talked for some time with the trader. "Oh, I just can't make up my mind," Jean said. "They have brought so many pretty things up the river!" Billy remembered what his father and mother had said about money growing on bushes and he said to Jean "Now sister, remember that silver foxes don't grow on bushes."

The trader got three good sized boxes and began adding up Jean's purchases and packing them away. Billy and Glenn turned their attention to stocking up on their own needs – cartridges, parts for dog harness, a few more traps, new boots, socks and shirts. A new pair of snow shoes as a Christmas present for Frank and skis for John; and the trader laughed as Billy told him why Frank needed new snow shoes. While Billy was interested telling about it, he didn't see Glenn select a fine hunting knife and slip it into the box after showing it to the trader behind Billy's back. The trader knew it to be a Christmas present for Billy from Glenn and he just nodded his head and wrote down the figures.

After Jean and the girl left the store to get ready for the dance, Billy and Glenn bought some things for her; scarf and sweater, sewing box, comb and mirror set and other things. They also got Christmas decorations and candles and some presents for their friends who had given them the puppy.

In one of the larger empty cabins the younger people at the post built a fire and put in a radio from the store and soon announced they were ready to dance. Billy and Glenn strolled over to their cabin, just as Jean and the other girl came running out looking very frightened. "Oh! That crazy old man," said Jean. "He was behind the cabin peeking in at us." Billy ran around the cabin but finding the old man had gone in the darkness he returned to the girls. "Who is he?" he asked the girl with Jean. "No one knows anything about him," she answered. "He doesn't seem to be a trapper, but he is mostly interested in dog teams. He has been here only a short time, everybody says he is crazy."

Billy did not have much fear that the dogs would be stolen. He knew the dogs too well for that and he grinned as he though of "Snow Boy" or "Ham-Bone" taking the patch out of the seat of the old man's pants, if he ever tried to take the sled or the dogs either. "Oh forget him," said Glenn "and let's go have some fun. Likely he has lived alone so long he just has queer ideas. I'd really like to talk more with him and see if he is as crazy as you think." "Well, that makes you crazy too," answered Jean, as they came into the cabin where the radio was doing it's best for the young people. The kids talked for a few minutes with others near the door and as a new tune came softly from the radio the boys swung into a waltz step with the girls.

The first hours of the evening the dance went on. Laughing, playing, singing and dancing, the young people were enjoying life as it was meant to be enjoyed. Some one went over to the post and brought back coffee, and things to make sandwiches. "Well its about time we were getting some rest," said Billy some time later; "Wonder where Glenn is, come to think of it. I haven't seen him for an hour." "I suppose he grew tired and went to bed," answered Jean "and I think I'll teach him some manners. He ought to know that young gentlemen don't leave their girls at a dance to walk home alone."

When Billy and Jean arrived at their cabin expecting to see Glenn sound asleep they looked only at an empty bed. Billy went over to the store thinking Glenn might be chatting with the trader, but he remembered that he had seen no light in the store when they walked over with Jean's girl friend. Not finding him there, he came back to the cabin. "The young Imp," muttered Billy – "I suppose he thinks this is funny. Think hard Jean, when did you see him last?" "Well," answered Jean "after we had all finished lunch together I saw him talking to that big trapper they call Uncle Jim. You know who I mean; he wears so much fringe on his buckskin jacket. They were both standing in the door way. Now suppose you think hard for awhile, yourself." "That is what I'm doing. I'm going to talk to this fellow Jim. If I can find him," said Billy as he started for the door. "He might be in the cabin next to the dog shed. I saw him come out of there this evening," Jean said as Billy went out into the night air.

Billy rapped several times on the cabin door and as it opened, he recognized the big man even in the darkness. Billy explained why he had come and the trapper who had been in bed for an hour, told Billy to come in and he lit a coal oil lamp. "I remember the boy very well," said the trapper kindly "and a right smart lad he is, but I'm sure I wouldn't know what became of him because I came over to this shack soon after I was talking with him." "Who else was around the doorway at that time and was anything said that might give us an idea where to look for him," questioned Billy with all the air of a detective. "Well say," answered the man, "have you by any chance seen a wild eyed, whiskered, old man around this Post?" "That happens to be who I'm thinking of right now," replied Billy. "What else, tell me." And the man began pulling on his pants and boots as he said, "That old scare crow was leaning against the corner of the dance cabin and I heard your brother say – " I wonder if there is any lunch left, I ought to give that poor old man a sandwich

Billy was thinking hard as the man finished dressing and turned to him. "Partner," and he placed a big hand on Billy's shoulder, "have you any dog that can track?" Billy squared his shoulders at the friendly gesture and replied, "Trapper! I got the trackinest dog that ever pulled against leather." "Then get him," said the big man as he buckled a heavy six shooter and belt around his waist, "cause I think you're goin' to need him!"

Dear Kids Has Glenn been kidnapped? Well don't worry about him and I'll see what can be done about it Daddy

Jean's note: No one in the family can remember why Daddy didn't finish this mystery. We are faced with only speculation. Perhaps as his employment with the U.S. Forest Service took more of his time, he was left too tired to continue his writing. We know that all of The Whoopenhollar Stories were written in the early to mid 1930's so the possibility that his job ended before he finished the story is not the answer. Maybe YOU would like to finish the story. With the possibility of Glenn being kidnapped, and he hasn't been found for 75 years; this could be a writer's delight! Go for it!

UNCLE FAY'S RANCH

May 30th 1935
Norwood, Colo

Dear Kids –

One nice warm spring evening there came a letter to the Whoopenhollar kids. Now these kids got lots of letters but this one was from their Daddy's uncle and it caused a real lot of excitement. And I'll tell you why! It was an invitation to spend a month or more on his ranch. Billy Whoopenhollar read the letter first to him-self and then to each one of the others, which was a lot of times as there are five of them you know – Billy – Frank – John, Jean and Glenn and then to make sure they all knew what was in the letter, Billy read it again to all of them put together.

I think that Jean was the most excited, because she put her toy frying pan on the dolls head and put the doll's hat on the toy stove, although Frank and John took the coal bucket out to the garden and brought the hoe in the house.

"When can we go," they all asked. "Well," said their mother. "I think you might as well go tomorrow and after you go I'll take a vacation myself and visit your Dad."

And so they all started helping their mother pack their clothes in a big trunk, or at least they thought they were helping. Each one wanted to pack a whole lot of playthings that their mother knew they wouldn't play with when they got to the ranch and so Mama Whoopenhollar did as much unpacking as anything else. It was late when the kids got to sleep that night – they had so much to talk about and finally their mother had to come up the stairs to make them be quiet. They thought that it never would come morning but sure enough it did just like it always does, and after breakfast they all got on the big bus, trunk and all. Their mother kissed them all goodbye and told them to be good kids and away went the bus to Denver.

After they arrived in Denver they had to go to the train station and get on a big long train. A man with a truck took their trunk to the station and put it in the baggage car. The kids learned a whole lot about trains that they never knew before. They found out that one car on the train was a dining car and another was the kitchen and when it was time to eat, a big friendly man who was the conductor took them into the dining car and they sat down to pretty little tables just like they have in a Cafe' and the big black engine kept right on pulling the train.

Sometimes the train stopped at towns along the way and here a few people would get off and sometimes other people would get on. The kids looked out the window of the car too, and watched the train men throw off lots of sacks of mail and still other sacks were put on.

"In the sacks they throw off are letters for the people in this town," explained Billy and in the sacks they put on the train are letters that persons have written here and are sending them to other towns." Glenn didn't understand this very well but then he was the youngest Whoop of all the Whoopenhollars.

After riding nearly all day on the fast train it finally came to the town where the kids were to get off and there was Uncle Fay with his big car to take them to the ranch. They all liked the ranch just as soon as they saw it and they wanted to get out and run around but their uncle said it was late and supper was waiting for them. And my! such a supper! All the eggs and butter and milk and other things they could eat

Uncle Fays' Ranch Hamlet, Nebraska

The next morning they were up bright and early – so they thought, but Uncle Fay said "Good morning sleepy heads, Breakfast is over now but perhaps we can find something for you to eat." "My goodness!" said the kids – "why even the sun hasn't been up very long." Then Uncle Fay said, "In the spring time on a ranch we can't wait for the sun, you know, because he is an old sleepy head too."

After the kids had had their breakfast their uncle started out with them to show them the place. What a big farm it was! The kids never knew a farm or ranch could be so large. Chickens were running loose every where and they saw some ducks, each one behind the other in a row. "They are going to the river for a swim," said their uncle. "I want to go for a swim too," John said. "O.K." was the reply "I know a swimming hole along the river where I used to go when I was a boy, but first, let us look around."

Soon they came to the horse barn and corrals. Frank peeked in the barn "Ah shoot! you haven't any horses, the barn is empty." Uncle Fay laughed, "the work horses are all out in the fields at work and the saddle horses and ponies are in the pasture, all except one which is in the corral. "Then why don't you let him out too?" Jean said. "I know," said Billy "You keep him in to ride after the other horses and bring them in." "That's right," was their uncles' answer. "The pasture is farther than you can see – too far to walk, but we don't always keep this same horse in the corral. They must take turns at that."

The kids wanted to see the barn even if it was empty of horses, because there were lots of things to see in there. In one place there were a lot of saddles and bridles and some harness too, although – most of the harness was on the work horses out in the fields and there were brushes to brush the dust from the horses and a medicine cabinet with medicine in it to give to them if they got sick. And there were bins for oats and corn and in the upstairs part was a lot of hay. This place Uncle Fay called a "hay mow." (loft)

Glenn peeked over the edge of a manger – you know a manger is where the horses eat their hay. Then there was an awful racket – "squawk! squawk!" "Wow!" Glenn hollered, even though Glenn was hardly as high as the manger, he could hollar about as loud as any of the Whoopenhollars. Out came an old hen just squawking like everything and when Glenn got courage enough to look in the manger again he saw an egg down in the hay "Before the horses come in at noon we will gather the eggs in the barn," said their uncle. "The cows are all out in the pasture too but let us go see the pigs." The kids followed Uncle Fay to where there were some very low long houses and a lot of pens. Before they got there, they could hear little squeals and grunts. Now here was a real sight for the kids. Some great big fat hogs and some little tiny pigs. "Which one of these little pigs went to Market?" Jean asked. Their uncle said "Jean, all these pigs will go to market, not one will stay at home. That is where you get all your nice bacon and ham and pork chops." John liked to see the big pigs stick their long noses thru the cracks in the pens. "They want something to eat," said the kids. "Yes," their Uncle Fay said. "They are always hungry and when they eat they get their feet right in the feed boxes and try to keep the others from getting any. That is the reason your mother has said that sometimes you kids were like little pigs."

The kids watched an old turkey gobbler spread his feathers and strut around. He looked just like the pictures that Billy and Frank had drawn in school for Thanksgiving Day. They thought he would make an awful big Thanksgiving dinner.

There were so many things to see that it was dinner time before they had time to feel hungry so gathering the eggs from the manger they walked up to the house. Just under the porch they saw something fuzzy move and when they crawled under for a better look, there were five little kittens – one for each of them.

They stood on the porch and watched the men bring in the horses that they had been working. The horses were thirsty and they drank a long time at the big water tank. Beside the water tank was a high wind mill and Uncle Fay explained that the wind blew the wheel around and around and this pumped the water into the tank. The kids wanted to know how they got any water when the wind didn't blow. "Sometimes we have to use a gasoline engine," he said, "but usually when the wind blows we pump enough water to last for three days and by that time, the wind will probably blow again."

After dinner Uncle Fay said "Now what would you like to do?" The kids could hardly wait to answer. "We want to ride on the ponies," they all agreed. So Uncle Fay said "O.K., you come with me." He didn't have to say it again for the kids almost got under his feet, all trying to get out the door at the same time and they raced down to the corrals. Uncle Fay went thru the barn and brought out a big saddle, the largest the kids had ever seen. This, he put on the horse in the corral and soon was galloping over the green pasture and out of sight. The kids tried to watch the pigs again and do a dozen other things but they just couldn't keep from watching the pasture and in a little while they saw the ponies coming with their uncle riding behind them. Billy and Frank ran to the corral gate and held it open while the ponies trotted in and then they swung the big gate shut. Such pretty ponies! Four of them and so gentle, too. They walked right up to the kids and stre(t)ched out their necks while the kids petted them. Their noses were so soft and warm, and smelled like the green grass they had been grazing in.

Uncle Fay brought out the saddles. There is one for each of you except Glenn and I will take him with me on my horse," he said. And so it was. When the kids had climbed into their saddles, Uncle Fay reached down and picked up Glenn with out even getting off of his horse. Glenn sat behind his uncle and held on to him. They rode out into the pasture again, and saw a few more horses and farther on were some cows and the cutest little calves, who kicked up their heels and ran behind their mothers. The ponies started towards the cows and the kids had to turn them away. "The ponies think you want to herd the cows home," said their uncle, "but we will go thru a gate soon and out into the field where the men are working.

Arriving at the edge of the field they sat on their ponies and watched the work horses, four abreast, coming down the furrow pulling a big plow that turned over two furrows at once. "That is a 'gang plow'," said Uncle Fay "and over here you see some more horses pulling a harrow, which is like a whole lot of rakes, and their uncle said, "We are planting oats here. See over there – those horses pulling that funny looking cart with the high wheels – that is a seeder and the man driving the horses is planting the oats."

"My, what a lot of oats," Billy said. "What do you do with all the oats that will grow on such a large field?" Of course their uncle said, "we use some to feed the horses and cows but most of it we sell to people who can't raise it themselves. Maybe some of the rolled oats that you will eat next winter will come from what we are planting here." "And what if none of the farmers would raise any oats or corn or chickens or cows or hogs or anything that all the people in the world eat?" asked Frank. "I'm afraid that you would all go hungry," said their uncle. "Then we are thankful there are lots of farmers," they all agreed.

"If you will come back again and visit me in the fall when the grain is ripe, I will show you how we cut it and haul it to market, but that is a long story and I'll let you see for yourself if you would like to come back again – and before you go home we will be planting corn and I know you would like to watch that," their uncle remarked. "And now it is too early to drive the milk cows home so we will ride clear around the pasture fence and see that there are no wires broken where the cattle and horses can get out."

And so the way they went (away they went) to the pasture fence with the ponies on a gallop. And after finding no holes in the fence, they turned their ponies towards the place where they had last seen the cows. As they rode near there they saw them away off in the distance, already starting for home themselves and with a Whoop and a Holler, the Whoopenhollar Kids gave their ponies a loose rein and they dashed off in hot pursuit.

Dear Kids – This will have to be continued when the Whoopenhollar Kids visit their uncle in the fall.

And now, be good kids. Lots of love from your
Daddy

Feb. 1936

THE WHOOPENHOLLAR KIDS

Uncle Fay's Ranch   2nd Part

"Hey Kids!" Whooped Billy Whoopenhollar from the back porch. "Come in and get ready, we're going to Uncle Fay's ranch." The other kids, playing in the yard, stood still for a minute, wondering if this was a new joke of Billy's. Then Jean grabbed up her doll and stepped on Frank's hand when he fell over the dump truck. But both reached the house about the same time. Johnny had to pour the sand out of his shoe, so didn't get there quite as soon and Glenn was last because he had to dig the sand out of his ear where Johnny had poured it.

No one knew for sure just what anyone else said in the next ten minutes, as all the Whoopenhollar kids were hollering at once. This is what the Whoopenhollar kids like to do best – all talk at the same time and when they have finished and found out that no one could hear them, they try it all over again, only a little louder each time.

"When do we start," they all wanted to know. "Just as soon as you get cleaned up and I can pack some extra clothes for you," said their mother. Now the Whoopenhollar kids just hate to wash their hands and faces but this was one time when they all wanted to use the wash bowl at once. The cat watched the soap suds fly with the most amazed expression and soon he sneaked out the door to take a look at the place, and finally making sure that he wasn't in the wrong house, he came back in, being careful to dodge the soap suds as he had learned from the kids to always keep away from soap.

By the time the big bus stopped by the door all the kids were ready and they gave their mother some big hugs and kisses and all said good by at the same time.

Soon the bus was rolling down the road and when the kids arrived in Denver and Grandma Whoopenhollar was right there to meet them and count them to be sure they were all there. And the next morning they got on another bus and road (rode) most of the day.

Now the summer was really over and the oldest of the kids should really have been in school, but their uncle had wanted them to visit him in the fall when the grain was ripe. The kids had been on the ranch in the spring and had seen the farmers plow and plant and now as the bus sailed along they could see field after field of grain and men were working there with big queer looking machines. "We will know all about those things when we come home next week," said Billy.

Do you suppose that Mama will be home when we get back?" asked Frank. "Oh of course," the others replied." "Where else would she be, – she is always home." "Well, I'm not so sure," said Frank and the rest of the kids looked worried. "I remember that she was packing some of her clothes in a suit case too." Fear began to show in the faces of the kids and they began to wonder what other kids do if they suddenly find themselves without any mother. Then Johnny began to grin "I'll bet I know," he said. "She is going to visit Dad and I think she was just as anxious to go as we are."

About the time the kids were beginning to tire of riding on tires, as riding a long way on some tires is tiresome, the driver slowed down to a stop. Lots of drivers pull up to a stop but this one slowed down. "This is as far as you kids paid to ride," said the driver, "so you will all have to get off." "Phooey to you from us," said the kids. "We didn't want to ride any farther, any place, any way, any how, 'cause there is Uncle Fay out there with his big car to take us to his ranch."

Uncle Fay was delighted to have the kids back again to visit him and when they arrived at the ranch there was the best supper for them all waiting for five hungry kids. "Now," said Uncle Fay, "we will get a good nights sleep and tomorrow you can help harvest the grain." "I will wind up the cat and put out the clock and we'll all go to bed."

The kids didn't go to sleep very soon as these kids always have so much talking to do and when morning came they were still sleepy, but they got dressed quicker than usual without having to be told as many times as they did at home.

After breakfast, they rushed down to the barns and Uncle Fay was there already fixing a pig pen. "You haven't as many pigs as when we were here last spring," said Jean "What happened to them?" "Something terrible happened to them," and their uncle looked so sad – "Something ate them up." "Oh, the poor little pigs," said Jean. "What do you suppose it was?" "Probably some boys and girls who liked pork chops," was their uncle's reply. "You see, I sold them when they got big and fat."

Frank watched the chickens and turkeys scratching around in the barn yard. "Didn't you used to have a pet peacock with lots of pretty feathers?" he said. "Oh yes, "and their uncle looked sad again. "We did, but the Peacock is dead too. You see it was like this: Your Aunt Lura had some colored Easter eggs left over and she put them in the old speckled hens nest, just for a joke. The hen told all the other chickens about it and they scratched the poor Peacock so bad he died." And their uncle wiped his eyes with his sleeve. The kids were sure it was a joke but when Uncle Fay looked that way, they thought it would be better not to laugh.

"Well, lets saddle up your ponies and we will ride out to the fields," he told the kids. I think the ponies were glad to see the kids too for they were already watching them thru the corral fence, or maybe it was because Glenn was poking some hay thru the fence.

Soon the kids were astride the ponies and clop, clop, clopping along towards a big field of wheat. Two men were in the field standing up the bundles of wheat into funny little piles. These bundles were tied around the middle with heavy twine. The kids heard a rattling noise and here came four big horses pulling a machine with a big paddle wheel on it. This was the binder that cut the grain, stem and all and then tied it up in bundles.

The man driving the horses stopped them and each Whoopenhollar kid took a ride with him around the field. Gee! It was fun to watch that machine wrap string around the wheat and then tie a knot in it.

Then as they sat on their ponies and watched, Uncle Fay spit out his wad of chewing tobacco and the horse he was riding gave a sigh of relief to be rid of so much load. After his mouth was empty Uncle Fay could talk better and so he started in. "You see, kids," he began, "after the wheat is cut we will stack it and then later on a threshing machine will come here" – "Oh," interrupted Johnny, "I know what they are, cause my Mama gave me one, once." Uncle Fay looked surprised. "She really gave you a threshing machine?" "No," was Johnny's reply. "Just the threshing."

As they quit laughing Uncle Fay went on – "When the threshing machine gets here, we will pitch these bundles from the stack into the machine and the straw will come out of one place and the wheat grains will come out of another. Some of this wheat will be saved for seed for next year but most of it will go to the mills where they will grind it up into flour or make wheat cereal out of it. We will do the same with the oats except that oats are used more to feed cattle and horses. The corn isn't ripe yet but we don't have to thresh it. We just pull the ears of corn from the stalk and later it is fed to the stock or shelled and ground up for corn meal or corn flakes."

As they rode on, Uncle Fay kept talking and soon they came to the river. "I have some fish lines set here," he said. "Lets get down and see what luck we have." He showed the kids the fish lines tied, one end to a stick and the other reaching into the water. One line was moving around in the water and when they pulled it out there was a big catfish on it. Catfish have sharp little horns and Uncle Fay showed them how to take it off of the hook. "We will take it up and have it cooked for supper," he said.

Uncle Fay-Team and Wagon

Every day Uncle Fay took the kids places and showed them new things and hardly before they knew it, the week was gone and it was time to go home. When they were all ready Uncle Fay took them in his car to the airport. "How would you like to go back to Denver in a big twin motored plane?" he said The way the Whoopenhollar kids used to whoop wasn't anything compared to the way they hollered when their uncle said that.

They all climbed up in the cabin of the big ship and after waving their good bys, the plane started off across the field and soon it was lifting itself in the air. Gee! it was fun to look down on the fields and farm houses that looked like Jean's doll things and Johnny's play ranch, as the plane roared thru the sky. It was hardly anytime at all until the kids could see the smoke and the tall smoke stacks of Denver and soon the big plane came gliding down at the airport in Denver. And there was Uncle Paul and Mamma there to meet the kids.

"Hi there kids," hollered Paul and Mamma "Hi, there folks," whooped the Whoopenhollar Kids. "Did you have a good time?" asked Mamma. "I'll say we did – and how."

This isn't much of a story kids but maybe I'll do better next time. Billy, I think it is about time that you wrote one for the rest of the kids . . .

Love from Daddy

DATES AND CAMPS WHERE RUTHERFORD WORKED

Written by Michael I. Smith, Grandson

Bill Rutherford: U.S. Forest Service Foreman, 1933-1942

In the spring of 1933 William Rutherford, with his wife Ethel, was raising five children in the tiny mining town of Georgetown, Colorado. Bill had recently sold off his portion of a freight-hauling partnership and he was trying to make a go of things in any way possible given the dire economic situation. A stint with the County Highway Department lasted just up to the moment a supervisor discovered that Bill hadn't voted properly in a local election. Other endeavors seemed equally doomed; in fact it would come to pass that the sale of his freight-hauling partnership would result in nothing more than an unpaid promissory note.

Needless to say, when the opportunity to work with the U.S. Forest Service cropped up, Bill jumped at the chance, though the fact that the work would keep him away from his family for weeks and months at a time must have given him pause and perhaps there were late night discussions between he and Ethel. Nevertheless, in the midst of The Great Depression folks did what they had to do in order to get by.

The sudden change in Bill Rutherford's employment prospects came about largely as the result of the creation of a single government agency during Franklin Roosevelt's first 100 days in office. The Civilian Conservation Corps was created with the goal of removing young men from our nation's roads, streets and highways, and placing them into the fields and forests to learn job skills and earn a little money. The CCC seems to have succeeded in accomplishing more of its goals than the raft of so-called alphabet agencies created to deal with the effects of the Great Depression and yet the C.C.C. is widely misunderstood or completely unknown to many Americans. One aspect of the program that has been especially overlooked is the impact the program had on the older men who served in the camps as military officers, camp superintendents and foremen as well as the impact these men had on the young enrollees in the program. Bill Rutherford was one such man. Bill Rutherford was a U.S. Forest Service foreman and supervisor. Bill Rutherford was my grandfather.

Late in his life Rutherford would recall that he began work as a Forest Service foreman in the third C.C.C. camp to be established in Colorado and he left the Forest Service while working at the last C.C.C. camp in Colorado.

In fact, between 1933 and 1942 Rutherford would work out of no less than seven main camps and countless smaller side or "spike" camps.

Initially posted to camp F-19-C near Waunita Hot Springs, Colorado, Rutherford lamented the fact that the enrollees assigned to the camp were all from out of state and unfamiliar with forestry work and even the rudiments of simple carpentry and construction. He noted in letters home that a camp in nearby Pitkin was finished constructing their quarters, despite the fact that its enrollees had arrived later.

Despite the enrollee's lack of field skills, they were eager to learn and eager to emulate the men placed in positions of authority. In one of his first letters home, written within two weeks of arriving at the Waunita Hot Springs camp Rutherford wrote:

> Among the ranks here the men call us "rangers." They often speak to us as "Mr. Ranger." They are mostly kids of course between 18 and 25 yrs. So it is easy to command their respect just in the difference of our ages. And when you add the name Ranger to us, which carries a romantic sound in itself, they are ready to accept us as an authority. It is amusing to note sometimes that we are being copied or the look of admiration they give us when we do what is to us the most common ordinary things ... This might give you some idea of how I have had to watch my own conduct, because we *must* stand at the head of these men or they are lost without a leader. When they have time on their hands around camp it is sometimes necessary to "shoo" them away from our tent so great is the attraction.

It is easy to see that Rutherford fast became more than a foreman and supervisor; Rutherford and men like him were mentors and father figures to some 3 million young men who passed through the ranks of the Civilian Conservation Corps. And let us not forget that the Forest Service of 1933 was not too far removed from the days when solitary forest rangers patrolled vast stands of timber, employing genuine field craft skills to deal with horses and pack animals, fence construction, blasting and explosives. Bill Rutherford brought into his service as a

Forest Service foreman his skills as a miner, wagon freighter and hunter. Consequently, he found himself in a varied series of job assignments in the C.C.C. camps.

At the Waunita Hot Springs camp, the primary work project involved construction of the Divide Road. At his next assignment, camp F-27-C, near Delta, Colorado in the Gunnison National Forest, Rutherford was assigned to work with crews to remove beetle-infested timber. On the back of a photo of he and his crew, Rutherford wrote, "The best bug crew that ever fell timber."

The Civilian Conservation Corps was set up so that work cycles or periods lasted six months. At the end of each six-month period C.C.C. companies were often rotated to new camps, often going to warmer climes in the winter and into the mountains during the summer months. Enrollees were chosen from the ranks of local relief rolls or through selection boards set up in smaller communities throughout the country. Often an enrollee's $25 allotment would mean the difference between going hungry and having food on the table. In one early letter Rutherford noted that, "The first lieutenant has a letter already from a mother of one of the deserters, begging him to reinstate the boy as his pay was to mean everything to her. You know the boys get $5 a month for themselves and $25 goes to their dependants." (As a government foreman, Rutherford's initial base pay was $150 per month.)

Rutherford's longest stint at any one area was spent in the San Isabel National Forest from the spring of 1937 to spring 1940. While in this area he was assigned to camp F-59-C at San Isabel, Colorado with the primary duty of supervising a blasting crew quarrying stone to be used in constructing the dam that would ultimately create Lake Charles. Rutherford spoke highly of men in his charge while on this project as well, writing in a letter home on February 14, 1938:

> I wish you could see the work now. I didn't fully realize how wrapped up I was in this particular job until this week. In fact I have been so busy training a force of men to do this kind of work that I'd forgotten to step off and really view the results until yesterday. I just sat with my back to the wind and watched this bunch of kids out on those ledges brace themselves against the

wind and tear into that hard rock. I haven't felt a love for a crew since I trained that bunch of boys in insect control work, until now. I believe I'd rather have a crew of green men to start in with if I can get the right kind, because I notice that each young sprout at this quarry is doing his work so near like I do it that it just seems like me doing it in 15 different places at once . . . I intend to tell the members of my crew that I'm proud to be head of a bunch like them.

Rutherford's sense of professionalism and concern for the men in his charge are evident when one reads the typewritten "Notice To Blasters" he prepared while operating the quarry at San Isabel. The notice stated tersely:

EACH BLASTER IS REQUIRED TO BE THOROUGHLY FAMILIAR WITH, AND ABIDE BY THE "DON'T" PREPARED BY THE INSTITUTE OF MAKERS OF EXPLOSIVES, A COPY OF WHICH IS INCLUDED IN EACH BOX OF DYNAMITE AND CARTON OF ELECTRIC BLASTING CAPS. WHEN YOU HAVE READ AND REVIEWED THEM HAND A COPY TO YOUR FELLOW WORKMAN. DON'T THROW IT AWAY. IT MIGHT BE THE MEANS OF SAVING HIS LIFE.

W.I. Rutherford
Foreman

It was while assigned to the San Isabel camp that Rutherford wrote and illustrated a how-to article on fence construction that appeared in the U.S. Department of Agriculture, Forest Service newsletter Construction Hints. Through a series of carefully rendered drawings and written descriptions, Rutherford told his readers how to build fences that were "horse high, bull strong and calf tight."

For all of the pride and professionalism that his work as a Forest Service foreman brought out in Rutherford, there were still occasions when the experience was far from smooth, especially in the initial months of the C.C.C. when the program was struggling to get off the ground organizationally. In an early letter Rutherford commented on the blandness of the food and added that the enrollees dining fare was often even more limited. Then, as if he'd suddenly remembered how lucky he was to have a steady employment situation in the midst of a national economic depression he quickly added, "While I think of it I should warn you not to broadcast any complaints I might make of our life here. It might make a difference in my future work. They simply don't want men or bosses who are not satisfied."

Organizationally, C.C.C. enrollees were under the command of the U.S. military only while in camp. During the regular workday, while out on the project, the technical service personnel had control of the enrollees. The technical services included the National Park Service, the Soil Conservation Service, the Bureau of Reclamation and of course the Forest Service, as well as a few other local and federal agencies. Naturally, when the technical services proposed that smaller side camps be established in order to accomplish work that would otherwise not be accessible to enrollees operating from a main camp every day, the military bristled. Side camps, the military brass argued, would take the enrollees out of the direct control of the military. Robert Fechner, the director of the program disagreed and establishment of side camps was begun immediately.

One of the first side camps Rutherford was tasked with setting up was the Hoffman Springs side camp, which was operated out of the larger camp F-48-C in Norwood, Colorado. "I have the swellest camp," Rutherford wrote home on August 24, 1935. "I'm surely king." Rutherford went on to explain how the tents were laid out in straight rows using a surveyor's instrument and that the forest supervisor visited and was proud of the side camp.

Between 1933 when the C.C.C. was established and 1942 when the program was disbanded, Bill Rutherford would oversee the construction of forest roads, the clearing of insect infested timber, the quarrying of stone and the construction of campground furniture. Additionally, he would conduct after hours sessions on native plants and vehicle maintenance and safety. Yet through it all, is wife and five children seem never to have been far from his thoughts and he yearned for the occasional opportunities to return to Georgetown for a visit. "It will soon be Glenn's birthday," Rutherford wrote in August 1936 from the Blue Lakes Camp in La Veta, Colorado, referring to his youngest son Glenn, poised to turn 4 years old that year. "I wish I could see him," Rutherford continued. "I'll send him a dime in this letter and he can buy anything he wants – up to 10 cents. That leaves me with 30 cents, but I don't owe anyone here now, and the check should be along pretty soon."

Despite his frequent and persistent lament that he wished his family could move closer to the camps, Rutherford was realistic enough to understand that such an arrangement would only be temporary, lasting only until he was assigned to the next camp. Ultimately, his wife Ethel and their children Billy, Frank, John, Jean and Glenn would remain in Georgetown, corresponding regularly and looking forward to the occasional visits. The U.S. entry into World War II found Rutherford assigned to yet another side camp, this time on Pike's Peak. The C.C.C. enrollees very quickly shipped out to the military or to take defense-related employment in the cities. The camp where Rutherford was assigned was converted for use as a camp for Mennonite conscientious objectors who were unable to serve in a military capacity due to the tenets of their religious faith. Rutherford continued to work as a foreman in charge of these work squads for a time, but perhaps noting a difference between crews who wanted to work versus crews who were being compelled to work, he decided to leave the Forest Service and return to Georgetown to seek employment in the revitalized local mining industry.

I don't know when I actually became aware of my grandfather and his life experiences; like so many pre-teen boys, I was somewhat oblivious to the stories of his early life in the Rocky Mountain West and I probably squirmed in my seat at the Sunday dinner table every time he started in with another of what I thought to be an endless stream of tales about mining, and freighting, and hunting and fishing and forestry.

Not until he was gone did I begin to have a real interest in the life of William "Bill" Rutherford, and then only in a particular nine year span from 1933 to 1942 – though all of his life was an adventure in hindsight. Sadly, I've discovered, too late, that the tales weren't endless.

Camp F-19-C, Waunita Hot Springs, Colorado, 1933. Foreman Bill Rutherford (L) helps his crew haul a log on the job site.

Rutherford poses beside a fence line, San Isabel National Forest, March 1936.

Fence Building Diagram

Camp F-59-C, San Isabel National Forest, Colorado.
This camp was one of about 7 primary Forest Service camps
that Bill Rutherford worked in between 1933 and 1942.

RUTHERFORD AND ECKLUND HISTORIES

WILLIAM E. (Old Billy) RUTHERFORD
1843-1923

William E. Rutherford was born to William and Mary Rutherford in Bristol, Addison County, Vermont, on May 7, 1843. He was an only child, born to them late in life. He was of Scots-Irish heritage, strong, hard working people.

His early life was spent at Bristol, Vermont where he received a good education finishing with one of the Vermont Colleges. In 1864, at the age of 21, in company with a friend, he came west to Brownsville, Nebraska. Here they equipped themselves with teams of oxen and crossed the plains to Denver where he engaged in mining for a few years. This would have been during the Gold Rush when gold was discovered less than ten years before at the junction of the South Platte River and Cherry Creek. Denver became a chartered city of Colorado Territory in 1861. During these years he crossed the plains twice with oxen encountering the danger of the early pioneers and being subject to attacks of hostile Indians.

William E. Rutherford-Central City, Colorado Territory

On Sept. 8, 1867 he married Elizabeth Rosenberry, to which union was born four children: Mary Adella, Anna Mabel, Willis Herbert (Daddy's father) and Edwin Fay. In 1868 he united with the Presbyterian Church.

William E. Rutherford and Elizabeth Rosenberry

Elizabeth, Mary Adella, William, Anna Mabel, Willis Herbert
1875

In 1870 at the age of 27 he and his family left Brownsville, Nebraska and moved to Pawnee City where he broke prairie. That is where the town of Burchard was at that time.

In 1876, about July 8th, or approximately two weeks after the Custer Massacre at the Little Big Horn river in Montana, Old Billy was westbound, somewhere in the northeastern part of Colorado, on the South Platte river, with his loaded freight wagon (drawn by ox-teams) which was a part of a general wagon train banded together for safety. They were about 50 miles out of Denver, about four or five days travel time with the wagons, when a small party of mounted Indians appeared on a distant knoll. Two riders immediately detached themselves from the wagon train to return soon with the report that the small Indian band were the only ones to be seen. No trouble was anticipated, the Indians dropped from sight, and the wagons rolled on.

Daddy was sorry that he couldn't tell all of us of a great Indian fight, but what actually occurred, he said was that as the wagons neared the knoll, the Indians again appeared, let fly a few arrows, then turned their ponies and fled. However, one of the arrows, nearly spent, had buried its sharp steel head in his grandfather's side just above the hip bone. It was pointed not at his stomach, but away from it. Just a little more force would have taken it on through the thin flesh of his side. Because of the barbs, it was more painful to back the arrow out than to take it on through, so making a slit in his skin with a hunting knife, he passed the arrow over his hip bone and out. It was passed down to Daddy, because he was the last male of the Rutherfords until he had sons. It has been passed to Old Billy's name sake, my brother Billy (Bill) and he has passed it to his only son, Burton William Rutherford.

Daddy gave this account along with a story about himself to correspondent Velma Michener, of the Georgetown Courier and it was published in the October 15, 1953 edition of that weekly paper. He showed the arrow and the steel head to her and went on to say that thousands of those heads were given to the Indians by the U.S. Government, when the buffalo herds were being scattered and depleted by the white man. Thus the steel arrow helped the Indian to procure his food and shelter at the very time when the killing of the buffalo by the whites was one of the methods used to subdue the Indians.

Brother Bill has told me that this is not a fact and needs to be re-told and given an accurate account. It was not the Government who supplied the Indians with these steel heads, but rather, it was the Traders, the people who operated Trading Posts. They are the ones who made the arrow heads. They were called "Trade Points." They were cut out of any old piece of steel that they could scrounge up, then hammered and forged into an arrow head. The Traders used them to buy things from the Indians. Bill is a voracious reader of facts, be it history or current and I completely rely on the accuracy of any thing he would tell me.

William I. Rutherford-100th Anniversary of the Arrow July 1976

In 1893 William F. (Old Billy) and wife Elizabeth moved to Hayes County Nebraska and there they homesteaded near Hamlet, then called Hudson. I don't know if his grown children were with them at the time of the move to the western side of the state, but probably. We know that their son Willis was there, because that is where he and Leaffie Stewart started their family. A few years after that, in 1899, Willis and Leaffie moved by covered wagon to Canon City, Colorado

The obituary of William E Rutherford tells us that he died in Hamlet, Nebraska on February 25, 1923, aged 78 years, 9 months and 18 days. He transferred his church membership (Presbyterian) by letter to the M.E. Church after coming to Hamlet in 1893. (I have been told that M.E. stood for Methodist-Episcopal) It was said of him: "His life in the community has endeared him to the heart of every one. As a husband and father, he was patient, loving and loyal. He left to mourn, his wife, three children, twelve grandchildren, six great grandchildren and a mother-in-law who find comfort in knowing God released his earthly bond in such a beautiful way, peacefully passing into the great beyond without a pain" His son, Willis preceded him in death due to the tragedy of being hit by lightning at age 30.

William E. and Elizabeth Rutherford
Hamlet, Nebraska

All of the above, I found from a print out of William E Rutherford's obituary. The obituary was given to Bruce Rutherford by Joan Lauenroth, County Clerk of Hayes County in 2006 when this research started. Joan is also a descendent of Old Billy. Her grandmother was his daughter, Mary Adella Rutherford Beezley.

WILLIAM IRWIN RUTHERFORD
1898-1978

Daddy was born William Irwin Rutherford on March 21, 1898 in Hamlet, Nebraska in a prairie sod house near the banks of Frenchman Creek. He was the only son of Willis Herbert Rutherford and Leaffie Stewart Rutherford. They were farmers. Daddy had four sisters – Nona, Nina, Fern and Mildred. Mildred died in infancy in 1904.

When Daddy was only a year old the family moved to Canon City, Colorado in a covered wagon where his father would work in the coal mines, take short surveying jobs and farm fruit orchards. His sisters, Fern and Mildred were born after they came to Canon City.

On June 4, 1904, a terrible tragedy took place that changed the lives of the whole family. With great appreciation to The Royal Gorge Regional Museum and History Center in Canon City, Colorado, I was furnished documentation of the tragedy, while writing this history. FROM THE CANYON CITY TIMES, DATED JUNE 9, 1904, HEADLINE: FATAL BOLT, comes this account: Bert Rutherford, a miner living on New York Avenue, South Canon, was struck by lightning Saturday afternoon at about 3 o'clock and instantly killed. Mr. Rutherford, in order not to disappoint his children in a promised picnic, went with three of them and little Ethel Gruitt (The Canon City Clipper named her Ethel Truitt) to Grape Creek Canon to fish in the DeWeese reservoir. Fearful of a threatening storm he was hastening home across the hills and when within half a mile from home near the fireclay mines was struck by a bolt. He was carrying a light steel pick and this might have attracted the lightning. The four children were stricken to the ground, a little boy having one shoe torn from his foot and sustaining painful burns. The current entered Mr. Rutherford's left temple and passing through his body made its exit through his left heel. It tore both shoes from his feet and set his clothing on fire, which was almost entirely consumed. The body was frightfully charred by the lightning and fire, which was still burning when discovered by a teamster alarmed by the frightened children who had recovered consciousness and were trying to reach home. Mr. Rutherford was about 35 years of age and leaves a widow and five children, the oldest but nine years of age. He owns his home but leaves little else as he was prejudiced against beneficiary or other insurance. He was a member of the United Presbyterian Church, was a kind father and was held in high esteem by his neighbors. His funeral occurred Tuesday morning, Rev. S. R. McLaughlin officiating.

When Daddy told us, as children, what he remembered about it, he said that when he saw what had happened to their father, he was crying and could not be consoled by his sister Nona. (He was only 6 years old) She told him that they needed to hurry home to tell their mother. He didn't want to leave his father. Nona told him to stop crying and said to him – "that could have been you, just stop your crying." They set off toward home. Daddy realized that the sole of one of his shoes was gone. The lightening had struck the nails that held the sole to the shoe and ripped the sole off. As they were walking, two railroad workers on a hand car saw them and asked where they were going. (The newspaper reported that a teamster had found them.) When they heard the children's story, they took them to their mother and they told her what happened. Then they took her to the scene. It was such a terrible time of grief for all of them and left the imprint of it on Daddy's mind for the rest of his life. Three months after this, baby Mildred died. Our Grandma Rutherford kept her family together by working as a care-giver to the sick and also as a mid-wife. It was a very hard life and they were extremely poor.

While Daddy was a very young boy, Canon City was well known as a location for the filming of silent movies. He was a handsome boy and was picked to do some bit pieces in several movies with Tom Mix. Tom Mix became an idol for him. Besides going to school and being in the movies, Daddy had a passion for learning to spin a rope and do rope tricks. By watching the professionals, he would practice for hours upon hours to learn. He became very good at it and never gave it up. He would spin ropes around us, as children and do fancy tricks for us.

Daddy finished eighth grade in Canon City, but his mother sensed that he needed the influence of a father figure and good hard work to help build his character, so she sent him to live with her people in Manitoba, Canada to work on their wheat ranch. He worked hard there but came back to his family for another year of school. He only completed nine years of school.

After this he went to Iowa and Minnesota where he worked on farms again. He was seventeen years old when he was in Minnesota While he was there he was hired to be in a movie, in which he wore a beautiful pair of angora chaps. He was hoping to get to do some spinning of his rope, but was not asked. It was a disappointment for him. Perhaps it was at this point that he realized how much time he had invested in practicing and it seemed at the time that it profited him nothing. He didn't know then that he would have five adoring children who would think he was the best rope spinner and performer of rope tricks that ever was!! Returning to Canon City once more, he took work on a cattle ranch near by, where he had been a chore boy during his school vacations. His riding ability improved, as did his roping, even taking part later in small town rodeos.

William I. Rutherford
July 4, 1915
Albert Lea, Minnesota

With the fall round-up of 1916 over, he went to work for the Empire Zinc Company as a sample boy in their mill near Canon City. He took ore samples from the various concentrators and prepared them for the assayers for a wage of $1.50 a day. He was eighteen years old by then. The ore came from mines paying $5.00 a day for miners – so he went to work at the mines.

There followed years of tramp mining. Some of the work was for a days pay and some was on contract and at other times it was leasing or prospecting. It took him to numerous towns and camps in Colorado, Utah and Nevada. The pay range was from less than nothing to $30.00 a day. He learned from all of this: general mining of ore, tunnel driving and logging work, carpentry and enough mechanics to overhaul his own car. He also learned blacksmithing, welding, tool dressing and a little business management. Because he liked to travel, he often took up jobs for a few days or weeks such as concrete paving in Ogden, Utah, and railroad shop work for the Santa Fe Railroad in Richmond, California. He did oil refinery work for Standard Oil of California, also road construction in Colorado. In Winnemucca, Nevada and Trinidad, Colorado he did some building construction.

I must explain what I meant by "Tramp Mining" In order to go from one mining town to another and from state to state, he and his partner, Bill Gardiner, a friend since childhood, had to catch rides on freight trains. They would grab on to a car as it was leaving a station and jump off before being caught when the train stopped again. The men who rode in freight cars, looking for work, were called "Tramps." Daddy told us stories of how they survived on very little food until they could find work. He said that once they had only two cinnamon rolls to last them a couple of days. Here is a funny little story I must tell: I invited Mamma and Daddy to have dinner with us. I was doing Fondue; cooking cubes of beef held on spears, in the fondue pot, when Daddy said," Jean, this reminds me of my Hobo Days!"

He was in Red Cliff, Colorado on November 10, 1918 when his draft board notified him that he had to report for service in the Army. He didn't get to do that, as the war ended the next day, (World War I)

In 1923 Daddy came to Clear Creek County with his mining partner, and child hood friend, Bill Gardiner. They worked for wages when necessary but preferred to lease a section of the diggings or contract their work for a percentage of the silver removed. For two years, A.G. Klein of the Red and White Grocery store in Georgetown, grubstaked the two Bills while they worked the Sunburst Mine for him, and prospected the Bard Creek area on their own.

One fine day in 1924, when he walked into Mr. Klein's grocery store, he saw his mother, who was keeping house for the two Bills. She was talking to a very pretty young lady that she had met at the Presbyterian Church. Mrs. Rutherford introduced the young lady to her son Bill. Quite taken by her, he got to know her. She was a senior in High School at the time. Her name was Ethel Ecklund. She was the daughter of Swedish parents and had lived all of her life in Georgetown. With permission from her parents, she began seeing Bill on a regular basis. They enjoyed hiking in the mountains around Georgetown which was something that Ethel had always loved to do. Bill taught her to shoot a gun, ride a horse and dance. Bill played on a baseball team and Ethel loved to attend the games to cheer for him and his team.

In 1925, Daddy and his pardner Bill were leasing a stope in the Belview Hudson Mine, just west of Lawson. The next year they opened up a vein of silver that paid them and the mine owners almost a weeks wages for every hour they worked. Knowing the fickle nature of silver veins in Clear Creek County, they sold their contract back to the mine owners while the mine owners were still more than happy to mine it themselves. After paying a long overdue grocery bill and other debts to Walt Anderson whose store in Lawson had been subsidizing their mining ventures, they went to Georgetown where they bought John Bieser's combined feed, fuel, freight hauling, logging and livery stable business located at Fifth and Argentine Streets. Ethel had graduated from High School by this time so Daddy asked her to be their bookkeeper. Shortly after that, Daddy asked Ethel to marry him

The name of the new business in town was "Gardiner and Rutherford." Hauling and logging was done mostly with horses. A large part of their work was ore hauling from mines in the Argentine and Greymont areas and freight hauling to the mines from the railroad depots in Georgetown and Silver Plume. They also cut ice on the Public Service dam above Georgetown in the winter and hauled it to the C. & S. Railroad depot storage building, which still stands at the corner of 11th and Rose St.

On September 25, 1926 Bill and Ethel were married in Denver at the home of Horatio Beavis, who was at that time the minister of the Presbyterian Church in Georgetown.

They moved into the Bieser house, which was acquired by Bill when he and his partner bought the Bieser hauling business. It is the house on Taos Street next door to the Old Missouri Fire House on the north side. While living there, they had two sons William Herbert (Bill) and Frank Edwin – later called "Buff."

William I. Rutherford-Ethel Ecklund
September 25, 1926

In October of 1929, the Stock Market crashed which led to bank closings, followed by businesses doing the same. Millions of people were without jobs. Many were unable to get their money out of the banks. This was the beginning of The Great Depression. Daddy and his partner had only been in business for four years when this terrible time in our history struck them down. They completely relied on the other business in town for their Livery Business to keep on going. Things just got worse and Daddy had to do something to provide for his family. Bill Gardiner was married but didn't have children. They made a deal. Daddy sold his half of the business to Bill Gardiner's wife, Ellen Trimble Gardiner, taking a promissory note as payment. Bill and Ellen hung on as long as they could, which wasn't long. They ended up just walking away from it, never paying Daddy a dime and moved to Oregon. Not only were they ruined financially but so was that long deep friendship ruined. Daddy was deeply hurt by it but very rarely spoke of it. He simply had to find a job so his family wouldn't suffer. He was never a slacker. He was a hard worker, who never showed signs of wanting to give up.

Having nothing, they moved into Ethel's parents duplex (Ecklunds) in 1930 and that year they were the parents of twins – Jean and John. Bill found work driving a truck for the

County Road Dept., he mined and prospected, raised large gardens, even rented vacant lots, plowing them to plant potatoes. Since his ex-partner's failing business still owed him money he had the use of a team of horses. Politics being what they are, one of the County Commissioners found out who Daddy had voted for in the recent election and he lost his job with the county.

In March of 1933 Bill was hired by the U.S. Forest Service as a construction foreman in the newly formed Civilian Conservation Corps, one of the government programs started by the new President, Franklin Delano Roosevelt. These work programs were called "The New Deal." This job was with one of the first C.C.C. camps in Colorado. When late winter came that year, he was out of work again because the camp moved to Oklahoma. He came home and went back into mining.

In January of 1934, Daddy and Dana Marshall of Georgetown began mining an extension of the famous Sunburst vein. They started opening up other old mines, near Georgetown, repairing buildings and what ever was necessary. Occasionally they went to other mining districts in the state to sample other prospects. These attempts to get a toe hold again in mining were discouraging so when the Forest Service offered him a job again, he went back to C.C.C. work as a foreman. This time he stayed on steady with the Forest Service.

His only assignment close to home was in 1938 for six months and then again in mid 1940 when he was construction foreman and training supervisor at the Idaho Springs, Colorado CCC camp. From that base camp, he and his crews improved the road up West Chicago Creek, built the camp ground and buildings at the end of the road and constructed hand-laid stone retaining walls along the road over Berthoud Pass. By this time many of the CCC trainees were Conscientious Objectors from the military draft. With the help of civilian volunteers, they planted trees at the old forest fire sites near Loveland Pass and cleared some of the early ski trails at Loveland Basin. The first lodge or warming house at

Loveland Ski Area was of log construction erected by the Idaho Springs CCC camp. It burned in 1946 and was replaced with one of the frame buildings from the then abandoned CCC Camp in Idaho Springs. In 1941 he was at a camp at Monument, Colorado when the camp was turned over to Conscientious Objectors and in August of 1942 he was in charge of these Objectors at Glen Cove near the summit of Pike's Peak. This was his last CCC assignment.

When the Civilian Conservation Corps was disbanded in 1942 because our country was heavily involved in WW II, Daddy was discharged from the U.S. Forest Service and came home to Georgetown. The U.S. Government was involved in efforts to increase production of strategic metals for the war effort. Lead and zinc were considered strategic metals, while gold and silver were not. Part of this was opening up old mine workings to determine if any recoverable minerals remained. Daddy went to work for the U.S. Bureau of Mines, and worked in the mines above Silver Plume, Colorado. The work was primarily to clear out old cave-ins to reach the inner workings where the most recent mining had been done. Nothing came of this, as the old-time miners had done a complete job of mining the old ore bodies to exhaustion. The operation was shut down after a few months.

June 28, 1943, he went to work for the Bureau of Prisons, Custodial Dept. at The Federal Correctional Institution in Englewood Colorado. A break from that job, and he and the two oldest boys, in 1945 worked for the U.S. Forest Service building a trail from the parking lot to the summit of Mt. Evans, using a horse cart to haul the gravel for the finishing of the trail.

After that short stint with the Forest Service, he returned to the Correctional Institution in Englewood where he taught leather tooling and was also a guard. He worked there for five years. He had learned the art of tooling leather while he was in the CCC's.

In the late 40's Daddy opened a shop in Georgetown, where the Red Ram Restaurant stands now. The shop was called Colorado Craft. He had studied more about leather tooling and became a true craftsman. His work was exemplary, because he knew how to tool into the leather to make a flower or leaf appear as though it was raised. He also used dyes that added to the contrast. He had orders from many places around the globe,

William I. Rutherford
Mount Evans 1945

making purses, wallets, belts, book covers and even saddles. Besides his leather art, he was also a fine shoe repairman. I don't recall why he had to close his shop. It must have been for economic reasons – or perhaps he needed to be in his beloved outdoor environment instead of confined to a shop, but for whatever reason he pursued yet another venture!

Because of his love of horses and with help from the boys who were all in high school by this time, he bought saddle horses and they ran a riding stable business out of our own back yard where we still rented the Manse. Daddy became actively involved with town activities and loved to help put on a rope trick show when asked. There was at that time a man named Ben Draper who had the great dream of reviving Georgetown. He planned wonderful events for the week-ends to bring in tourists and help the economy of Georgetown. Even though Daddy didn't pursue trick roping as any kind of a career, he was very good at it, because he had practiced so long and hard when he was a kid. He would do tricks for us when we were little. We were his adoring fans

In 1953 he went to work at Lookout Mountain School for Boys in Golden. He taught leather craft there and did the shoe repair for the boys, teaching it as well. About 1956 he persuaded Mamma to give up the Presbyterian Church Manse that our family had occupied for twenty-three years, and move to Golden to the school where he worked. They lived in one of the apartments on campus and started a new life. Mamma was forty-nine years old and it was the first time she had lived away from Georgetown in her entire life, except for a brief time when she was a little girl and her family lived in Salina Kansas. Daddy retired in 1963 and was free to live the life he longed for.

They moved to Ft. Collins where they had a small trailer on son Bill's property where he had his beloved horse Penny and a wonderful garden. He could take off whenever he got the notion and spend a whole day fishing in the lakes near by. Horsetooth Reservoir was one of his favorite places. He always had Mamma with him and they did so enjoy this new life together. He kept his garden weed free, but when fishing season opened, he let the weeds have their way!

William I. Rutherford with Penny
Continental Divide 1958

On March 20, 1978, the day before his 80th birthday, Daddy and Mamma flew to Arizona to visit me and my family. Daddy was not well when they came, having just come out of the hospital in Denver recovering from a slight heart attack. His doctor was delighted that he wanted to come here for a visit instead of returning to the high altitude of Colorado. As it turned out, he was in and out of the hospital here, in Sun City, actually, several times during that year and was never able to return to Colorado. He passed away on December 31, 1978 at the age of 80 years, and 9 months. His body was returned to Colorado. His funeral was held at the Presbyterian Church and he is buried at Alvarado Cemetery north of Georgetown.

NOTE: Bill's history of his nine years with the CCCs, written by Michael I. Smith, his grandson is included in this book. Michael has spent the past fifteen years researching and writing about the days of "The CCC's" He is, at the time of this writing, President of the Phoenix, AZ Legacy of the C's and is a Board Member of the National Legacy of the CCC's

ECKLUND HISTORY

Mamma was born Ethel Edith Marie Ecklund on Sept. 13, 1907, in Georgetown, Colorado, the first born child of Frank Emanuel Ecklund and Emma Jemimah Richt, Ecklund. That name was changed to Ricketts, probably when registering at Ellis Island, after the family had arrived from Sweden. They also had a son, Paul Ecklund, who was born in Georgetown, as well, on May 27, 1912.

Frank E. Ecklund was born on a farm near Smolan, Kansas, on Jan. 18, 1874, the third child of Swedish immigrants who had come to the United States and settled in that place in Kansas in the mid 1800's. His parents were Frans August Eklund, born Aug. 30, 1838 and died Mar.19, 1915; Mathilda Carolina Swenson Eklund born in 1842 and died March 17, 1877, only 35 years old. They had two daughters, Amanda and Marie and one son, Frank, who was only 3 years old when his mother died. Their father, Frans, raised his children in a devout Christian home and never remarried. Note here that the name was spelled Eklund when they immigrated to this country, but for some reason, and I don't know why, at this writing, our Grandpa Frank spelled it Ecklund. Frans and Mathilda are buried in the Salemsborg Lutheran Cemetery four miles south of Smolan.

When our Grandpa (Frank) was in his early 20's, he had to leave Kansas because of a chronic asthmatic condition. Seeking a higher altitude, drier climate and a location away from the harvesting of hay, he went to Georgetown, Colorado He hired on as a laborer at the Waldorf mine. While working at Waldorf, he bought a book on blacksmithing and tool sharpening. This would be the profession in which he later became a master. "Through a combination of practical experience and self study, he became a professional blacksmith and carpenter. He would follow these two occupations all his life" This is a quote from a piece that Bruce Rutherford, great-grandson wrote after having a question-answer time with his Grammie, Ethel Rutherford.

When Frank began his new life in Georgetown at the turn of the century, he took room and board at The Ennis House and at times, The Barton House, both hotels of that era located at the south end of town. The Ennis House was located at Fifth and Taos Streets on the NE

Frans August Ecklund Family
Smolan, Kansas 1888

corner. Straight north at the SE corner sits the old commercial building that was once known as the business of J. Snetzer-Merchant Tailor. The Ennis house was gone before The Great Depression days. The Barton House stood at the top of the hill until it was leveled in the late 30's to build the new school, built by the WPA-one of the New Deal Programs. The Snetzer building, called McCurdy-Snetzer building, still stands and has been restored. When we were kids, Mrs. McAdams lived there. She used to own the Hotel DeParis. She was also a school teacher and taught brother Bill before she retired.

One story passed down is that Frank attended a Swedish picnic in Denver where family and friends had gathered, and there he met young Emma Ricketts who had come to Denver from Sweden with her mother in 1894. Another version is that young Emma came by train to Georgetown to visit friends and met Frank. I don't know which story is the true one. After a long engagement, because they were second or third cousins, they married in Salt Lake City on June 28, 1906 because that state permitted the union. They took up residence in a little white house on Biddle Street, which later became known as the Rarey house. Frank continued to work at Waldorf where he was now the mine blacksmith.

Frank Ecklund and Emma Ricketts
June 28, 1906

Ecklund Home in Georgetown

Frank Ecklund
Blacksmith Shop at Waldorf

On September 13, 1907 their first child was born – a girl that they named Ethel Edith Marie – she was our Mamma. On May 27, 1912, they had a son, Paul Emanuel, our Uncle Paul! Both babies were born at home in that little white house.

Ethel Ecklund
1909

In the Spring of 1921 they moved from Biddle Street to the house where they lived the rest of their lives – 927 Rose Street. That same year, Frank accepted an offer from Lawrence Anderson to work his mine at the head of Crystal Creek. That summer he and his partner Oscar Nelson, built a cabin and a blacksmith shop on Crystal Creek below the mine. I am going to quote my nephew Bruce Rutherford's writing about that cabin. This was taken from an essay he wrote while still in school, probably about 1974. "FRANK ECKLUND WAS MY GREAT GRANDFATHER. THE CABIN HE BUILT STILL STANDS, THROUGH 53 WINTERS AND TEN FOOT SNOWS, SIXTY MILE AN HOUR WINDS AND BELOW ZERO TEMPERATURES. AND NOW I GO THERE NOT TO CUSS THE COLD, WIND AND SNOW, THAT MADE MINING IMPOSSIBLE, AS HE DID, BUT TO ENJOY THE COMMON CHORES THAT HE HAD TO DO TO LIVE IN THE CABIN IN THE WINTER." Bruce not only went there on occasion, but after graduating High School, he lived there with his dog Tater. He walked down the trail every day and drove to Georgetown to go to work, and returned at the end of the day.

Frank, Ethel, and Paul
Anderson's Cabin
1923

Frank worked at many mines in the area, including the Sceptre, Boston, Moline, Dives Pelican in Silver Plume and at Waldorf. He would walk to his job every Sunday afternoon and back home again Saturday afternoon, Waldorf being the farthest – 8 miles.

Frank lived to be only 67 years old. He died of congestive heart failure in a hospital in Denver on December 7, 1941 – The day of the Pearl Harbor Attack

Grandma Emma Jemima Richt was born in a little country village in Sweden by the name of Molen, Bredestads Parish, Jonkopings County, Smoland District, on November 27, 1874, the same year as Grandpa. Her parents were August and Anna Charlotta (Nelson) Richt. Emma was the youngest of five living children – four had died in infancy. Her brother Carl and sisters Clara, Olive and Hannah left Sweden to come to America to make a better life. When their father August died in 1894, Anna brought Emma, then nineteen years old, to America to join the rest of her family in Denver. They departed from Southhampton on Oct 1,1894 on a ship named The Berlin. They never returned to Sweden. They all had entered through Ellis Island in New York.

August and Anna Charlotta Richt
Molen, Sweden

Carl started a candy factory in Denver, which later became Brach's Candy. Carl never married. He was engaged to a girl named Edith Roman., but she died and he never found another to take her place. Grandma Emma loved Edith and looked forward to her being her sister-in-law. Mamma's second name is Edith, named for Uncle Carl's love. All of the girls worked as domestic help in the nice homes in the Capital Hill district of Denver. Olive moved to California to do domestic work. She later returned to Denver where she lived with her sister Clara. Neither of them ever married. Hanna married John Larson and lived in Haywarden, Iowa where they farmed. They had one daughter, Margaret.

Emma and Frank Ecklund
Carl Ricketts and Edith Roman

Grandma (Emma) spent her life, after raising Mamma and Uncle Paul, helping our family. She was the most perfect Grandma in every way. I can still see her leaving our house in the afternoon carrying a bag of our stockings with her. After she fixed supper for Grandpa and did her own house work she sat and darned the stockings in the evening.

Uncle Paul went to work for Public Service Company of Colorado, immediately after graduating Georgetown High School in 1930. He was employed with them for forty seven years. In 1938 he met Wilma Strole who was here from Kansas visiting her sister, Mrs. Dana Marshall (Marie). They were married July 26, 1939. They had three children: Paul Richard was born June 20, 1941. He is married (Lois) with two sons. They live in Ithaca, NY where he is a professor at Cornell University. Linda Fae was born December 1, 1949, was married to Greg Williams and has two daughters. Linda lives in Lakewood Colorado. Jeanne Marie was born June 25, 1956 and lives in Indiana with her husband Pat Ryan. Jeanne has a son from a previous marriage, (Shepard) named for his grandfather, Paul. It was very exciting when Uncle Paul married Aunt Wilma and started a family. We had never had any cousins that lived any where near us. By the time Dick (Paul Richard) was born I was already eleven years old, but Aunt Wilma used to let me take him to the park in his stroller while she did the laundry.

Paul and Wilma Ecklund, Frank and Emma Ecklund,
Ethel and Bill Rutherford
Georgetown, Colorado 1940

Grandma loved music and used to sing little Swedish songs to us. She was so fun loving She surely was content spending her life taking care of Grandpa, who was in poor health, tending her gardens, keeping her little house neat as a pin, baking good Swedish things and still spent hours at our house helping with the work. I learned much from her and loved hearing her stories about life in Sweden – especially when she talked about mid summer when daylight never ended and night never came. As a young girl she and her friends loved to be out on the lake in a boat. She played the mandolin, others played their instruments and they sang. She told me that even though they stayed out late because it wasn't dark, they still had to go to work the next day. I never did ask her what kind of work she did. I didn't think to ask. She was nineteen when she left there. Very shortly after coming to Denver in 1894, she bought a guitar which she played. When my brother Bill was grown, and had taken guitar lessons, she gave it to him. He also played it, but now he has passed it on to his daughter Lynn and still that guitar is being played, making beautiful music. Lynn played it for us at our family reunion in 1994 and she and her two daughters, Heather and Jennifer, sang. The guitar was 100 years old at the time of that reunion.

Grandma had to spend some time in a nursing home in Denver because Mamma was not able to lift her and take care of her. A lady in Georgetown offered to care for her so she was able to get back to Georgetown. I was so afraid that she would pass away while I lived in France – but she lived two more years after my return. She died April 12, 1957. She and Grandpa lived their entire married life in Georgetown, except for a very brief stay in Salina, Kansas. Grandma was a widow for sixteen years. They are both buried at Alvarado Cemetery. north of Georgetown.

Quick Coffee Cake

1 or (3/4) cup sugar
1 1/2 " flour
2 tsp baking Powder.
1/4 tsp salt.
1/4 cup butter or oleo softened.
1/2 cup milk.
1 Egg - well beaten.

Sift dry ingredients together, work in softened oleo. Add egg & milk. Pat into an 8" square greased pan. Sprinkle with mixture of 1 tsp Cinnamon & 2 tsps sugar. Bake 20 min in moderate oven.

Ethel Ecklund's Quick Coffee Cake
Original Recipe

"My Little Girl"
Sam M. Lewis 1915

EPILOGUE

The Whoopenhollar Kids Grow Up

Billy — William H. Rutherford graduated high school in 1945, was drafted into the U.S. Army and after his tour, he enrolled in Colorado Aggies, on the G.I. Bill. Aggies is now Colo State University. After earning a Masters Degree in Wild Life Biology he was employed by Colo State Game and Fish Dept. Bill retired from the Dept. after 32 years. Bill married and has two children. He and his wife, Clarice are retired, living in Ft. Collins, Colorado.

Frankie — Frank E. Rutherford has been called "Buff" since he was a young teenager. After he graduated high school in 1946, he joined the U.S. Army and served eighteen months. Having signed up for the Reserve, in the fall of 1950 he was called to serve during the Korean War After discharge he attended Colorado Aggies in Ft. Collins on the G.I. Bill of Rights. Buff married, had three children and was the Assistant Manager of Loveland Ski Area for 30 years.

After that, he and his wife Mary Lou owned and operated a horse drawn carriage business in Georgetown for twelve years. They still reside in Georgetown where Buff creates art from used horse shoes. The pieces of work are called Sculptshoes and can be found for sale in the local shops.

Jean Emma Jean Rutherford graduated high school in 1948, attended Colorado Women's College, and was employed by Mountain Bell Telephone Co. in the accounting department. She married, lived near an AF.Base in Chateauroux, France for nearly three years. Her first child was born there. Mostly, her career was in banking. She has three sons, is now widowed and has been living in Arizona for over thirty years. Jean worked in later years as a care giver to the elderly making, it possible for them to remain in their homes. She enjoys her family, volunteering in her small community and in her church.

Johnny John Paul Rutherford graduated with Jean in 1948, after a brief enlistment in the Army Air Corps in 1947. He was injured during Basic Training and was given a Medical Discharge. He attended Oklahoma Baptist University but was unable to continue as he lacked funding. John was always innovative and smart. He was hired by Hannah Rubber Co. in Kansas City, Missouri where he later became Office Manager. He was also employed at Gates Rubber Co. He was a one-of-a-kind industrial rubber fabricator and was a valued employee. He married and had three daughters. He retired in Kansas City. There he helped his wife Glena with her beautiful gardens, traveled and enjoyed their grand children. He died of cancer at age 68.

Little Glenn Glenn F. Rutherford graduated high school in 1950, enlisted in the U.S. Navy, where he received his education in electronics. This served him well after his discharge from the Navy. He found employment with the Gas Company in Denver and later with Martin Marietta. for several years. He had three children from his first marriage, one of which was born in Hawaii while in the Navy. He re-married later and had four more children.. Becoming tired of living in the city, he and his family moved to Columbine Lake, near Grand Lake, Colorado where he was employed by the HOA to maintain the community buildings, swimming pool, roads, and keep properties safe. Glenn and his wife Sue are living a retired life style in Brownsville, Texas